STRAIGHT TALK
WITH GAY GUYS

What Girlfriends Can't Tell You
and Straight Men Won't

DAYLLE DEANNA SCHWARTZ

Health Communications, Inc.
Deerfield Beach, Florida

www.hcibooks.com

Library of Congress Cataloging in Publication Data

Schwartz, Daylee Deanna.
  Straight talk with gay guys : what girlfriends can't tell you and
straight men won't! / Daylle Deanna Schwartz.
     p. cm.
  Includes bibliographical references and index.
  ISBN-13: 978-7573-0576-4 (trade paper : alk. paper)
  ISBN-10: 0-7573-0576-8 (trade paper : alk. paper)
  1. Man-woman relationships. 2. Dating (Social customs)
3. Mate selection. I. Title.
HQ801.S43973 2007
306.73082—dc22   2006039586

HCI, its logos and marks are trademarks of Health Communications, Inc.

Publisher: Health Communications, Inc.
          3201 S.W. 15th Street
          Deerfield Beach, FL 33442-8190

Cover design by Roxanne Daner
Inside book design and formatting by Dawn Von Strolley Grove

STRAIGHT TALK WITH GAY GUYS

This book is dedicated to my good friend
Brie Austin,
for your help with this book and
for your terrific support in general.
I send BIG thanks to you for being there for me!

This book is also dedicated to my prayer
that as people get more enlightened,
there will be more acceptance and
appreciation for all of God's children.

CONTENTS

ACKNOWLEDGMENTS

As always, I must begin by thanking God for all of my blessings. Without my strong belief in Him, I wouldn't be where I am today! My many blessings include all the people who were instrumental in bringing this book to fruition.

Thank you, June Clark, my agent at Peter Rubie Literary Agency, for your belief in me and for all your hard work on my behalf. Thank you to all the people at Health Communications, Inc., especially Michele Matrisciani, my editor, for your strong confidence in my book; Kim Weiss for your great instincts and support for the promotion of this book; Katheline St. Fort and Carol Rosenberg for your diligence and attention. And a special thanks to Peter Vegso, founder of Health Communications, Inc., for welcoming me so warmly into his wonderfully unique company. I appreciate all the support from everyone at HCI!

It's hard to find the right words to express my appreciation for the thirty-three guys who shared their advice with me for this book. Interviewing them was a joy! They sincerely wanted to help enlighten women about how to be more powerful and in control of themselves. And so, for their time and thoughtfulness, I say a great big THANKS to Michael Alvear, Michele Antiga, Kevin Aviance, Kyle Barton, Brian Belovitch, Kenny Bonavitacola, Travis D. Bone, Randall David Cook, Randy Dotinga, Michael Thomas Ford, Kevin Kelly, Fritz LaBoucane, Hedda Lettuce, Matthew Link, Michael Luongo, Dan Matthews, Michael McDerman, David Paul Miramontes, Michael Musto, Vinnie Petrarca, Yiannis Psaroudis, Ed Razzano, Andy Reynolds, Alex Romero, Kevin Scott, Patrick Sherman, Curt Smith, Jason Stuart, Carl Sullivan, Rick Trabucco, Keoni Udarbe, Glenn Wiehl, and Bob Witeck. It's been so much fun to write this book because of how special you are. I love you all!

Several people went out of their way to help me with this book. Thank you again, Randy Dotinga, for stepping up to put me in touch with many of these great guys when I first decided to write this book and for your continued support. Thank you again, Bob Witeck, for being such a sweetheart with your delightful, upbeat encouragement. Thank you, Mitchell Waters, for your strong support and friendship. Thank you, Rochelle Joseph, for sharing your gay friends with me and for your persistence at the final hour.

Big, big THANKS to my wonderfully supportive family. And thanks to my friends who supported me through my growing pains and education about men. Thank you, Ellen Penchansky, my best friend in the whole universe, for always cheering me on as I found my way to a happy life, with or without a man. Thank you, Julie Coulter, for your constant cheerful love and encouragement. Thank you, Nasrin Sahihi, for being such a good friend by e-mail from Tehran.

A special thanks to everyone at the Moonstruck Diner on Second Avenue and Fifty-eighth Street in New York City—where I regularly take my laptop out for a yummy meal and lots of coffee refills with terrific service from my special waitress, Hedia.

INTRODUCTION

I used to be a jerk magnet. My need for a man kept the word "selective" out of my vocabulary. Happiness was also missing, but I was too busy coping to realize it. That was in my days of low self-esteem, lack of spirituality, and the strong belief that I was nothing without a man. I tolerated intolerable behavior, rather than risk losing my latest HIM—who I made larger than life, the tune to my dance, the center of my world, and my top priority. I waltzed for each jerk but cried when I was alone. They sucked me dry as I willingly acquiesced to their needs. Complaining to my girlfriends made it worse. They were as needy as me and encouraged doing things based on their own anger toward men, or a belief that we should stick it out with any available guy.

When desperation set in, I got a haircut. Sure, some women turn to their girlfriends for support when they have problems with men. Some turn to food. Some get the latest book on how to handle a man. When I used to feel out of control with guys, I got lots of haircuts. Then I would talk to Larry or David about my current guy—

and get the best advice. Compared to my girlfriends' outlook, my best gay guy friends' perspectives were priceless because while they were outside of the hetero dating scene, they were able to offer perspective into the male mind but keep the focus on MY well-being. They think like men but also deal with the frustrating male dating behavior and attitudes. Gay men see both sides of hetero dating, so they can offer helpful suggestions and real advice from the trenches. After getting straightened out by my gay hairdresser, I felt refreshed, enlightened, and more in control for a while—with shorter hair.

My gay guy friends finally woke me about how to handle myself!

The most exhilarating feeling on Earth is to be in a win/win situation with guys! I win if I'm with one who makes me happy. I win if I leave one who makes me unhappy, because I control my own happiness now and have a life to return to after a breakup. In my book, *All Men Are Jerks Until Proven Otherwise*, I provide insight on how to put the importance of men into perspective, illustrated by interviews with everyday people. The response from women has been very positive, so I decided to take my advice a step further. For this book I turned to reliable sources that have always worked for me. Instead of interviewing straight women and men, I approached thirty-three smart, observant, and caring gay men to help me enlighten us even more.

Why gay guys? These insightful guys have an inside view and can give you the REAL picture because they interact with men the way we do—but still think the way straight men do on many levels.

Gay guys were brought up with the same male stereotypes as straight ones and deal with a lot of the same issues and ways of handling situations. When a woman has a gay friend, he's usually the one she turns to for dating or relationship first aid. Dan, whose many girlfriends include Pamela Anderson, explains:

> 66 More than half of my friends are straight women. I always find a lot in common with them. Sometimes we're after the same thing, but we're not in competition. As a result, there's this wonderful camaraderie. 99

Gay guys also tend to be more realistic than our girlfriends are. They deal with our tears yet keep a practical perspective on a situation. And since gay guys date men, they have insight on that level, too. Gay guys see things in ways that women can't, and that straight guys aren't evolved enough to recognize or don't want you to know. Most gay men hear the same yammering about straight men issues from their own girlfriends that I hear from my readers and have guided them to finding resolutions. They know our patterns and are straighter in addressing them. Implement their input to grow as a healthier woman and take control of YOU with men.

Many gay guys are straight chick magnets, with loads of female friends who cry on their shoulders and welcome the practical advice given. The wonderful characters on the long-running TV show *Will & Grace* are an example of how advice from a gay friend is like no other. While gay guys are more sensitive and more straightforward in their assessment of a situation, they're still guys and part of the man club, and they're going to let us in!

Let's face it: We often need that swift kick in the ass to stop our moaning and complaining—and defending HIS inexcusable behavior. And this kick is what I and the thirty-three men involved in this book hope you will get out of this. You won't find step-by-step "get that man" techniques, nor is this a self-help book that analyzes your dating behavior in a psychological way. This is just real reactions to some of our actions when it comes to figuring out guys, what they want, and how we should or should not think about any perspective mate. The advice is what you'd hear over a three-martini dinner with your gay guy friend. The mission of this book is to help you change your response to men in a way that will empower, not frustrate you.

Don't have a gay friend? Well, you've come to the right place. Now you have thirty-three, and they won't hold back what they want you to know! Where did I find guys to interview for this book? They come from all over. Some have been in relationships with, or were even married to, women. Others are insightful in their observations because they have experience hearing women complain about scenarios that have driven them crazy time and time again. I made sure to enlist the help of guys with female friends who come to them regularly with guy problems. They were excited to advise women for this book and were more than happy to share perspectives on straight relationships.

"Gay dating is NOT that much different than straight dating."
—Michael McD

This book has a positive outlook on men. While I don't care for some of their behavior, in general, I adore men and believe that many of their actions are caused, or at least facilitated, by our expectations and responses to them. Many do jerky things because they can. If you allow a guy to take advantage of you, why shouldn't he? It's human nature to take when someone gives, or to do what suits you, if you're allowed to. YOU have to change, not your guy. The way you handle yourself determines how he treats you, and if needing a man is what drives your behavior, you'll put up with all sorts of nonsense. That doesn't make the guy a jerk. It's up to you not to accept unacceptable behavior.

The guys and I want to show you how you can change your response to men, which can get you more of what you want. You shouldn't change who you are for anyone! But if you change your attitude, you can take control of YOU. Men are NOT jerks because they don't live up to (a) the expectations that you and your girl-friends create, (b) the fantasies that movies and books portray, or (c) the larger-than-realistic importance you give them. If you put the importance of men into perspective and recognize your own importance, you have a good chance to experience the kind of joy I've let into my life. Yes, I let it in. But it didn't just happen. I had a lot to learn, and you can learn the very important lessons, too: One woman's jerk can be another woman's treasure. By replacing desperation and games with a positive attitude about yourself, guys will have no choice but not to be jerks, if they want you to stay. What a concept for many of us—being in the driver's seat!

With my gay advisors as your guides, you can attract a guy who is healthy for you. When you focus on creating a happy life based on YOU, not on whatever HIM you find, you stop being a jerk magnet. Then, life becomes more beautiful. A win/win relationship can be yours! The guys and I want to show you how to achieve the kind of happiness that's worth going after.

This book begins by enlightening you about how we create many of the jerks we later complain about. The main focus is on constructive ways to become an empowered woman. At the end of each chapter I provide First-Aid Tips you can use immediately as you go out into the world with your newfound perspective.

Disclaimer: Nothing that we say is meant to make you feel guilty or hate yourself. Let this book be a wake-up call, not another source of issues. We've all gone through many of the things the guys and I speak about. While you may recognize yourself in our examples of how women do things that attract jerks, please don't beat yourself up over it. We beat ourselves up over enough things. Put your energy into being loving to yourself, so you can find your way to having control over how men treat you.

MEET THE GUYS!

I n my quest to provide a taste of the joy of getting advice from gay friends, I interviewed a variety of fabulous gay guys for advice. I include them here so you can refer to the list if you want to see who's giving what advice. They're alphabetized by first names to make it easy to reference each one. In the case of men with the same names, I include their last initial and, in the case of the Michaels, a bit more.

Alex Romero is a graduate of Yale University with a degree in biology, currently working as a recording artist in NYC.

Andy Reynolds is president of Penetration, Inc. in New York City, doing PR, production, and management.

Bob Witeck is former press secretary in the U.S. Senate, a public relations executive, and cofounder and CEO of his public relations firm, Witeck-Combs Communications, Inc. in Washington, D.C. (clients have included Christopher Reeve Foundation, American Airlines, IBM, and more). Bob also coauthored *Business Inside Out* (Kaplan Business, 2006)—marketing to gay consumers.

Brian Belovitch is assistant photo editor for *People* magazine, based in New York City.

Carl Sullivan is a magazine editor and journalist from Brooklyn.

Curt Smith is a photographer who was raised in Tennessee and now lives in Florida.

Dan Matthews is a PETA activist in Virginia who campaigns closely with women such as Pink and Chrissie Hynde. His international exploits for animal rights, especially those undertaken with Pam Anderson, who calls him her gay husband, are brought to life in his irreverent book, *Committed* (Atria/Simon & Schuster).

David Paul Miramontes owns the David Paul Salon in Beverly Hills, California, and has done hair for many celebrities.

Ed Razzano represents songwriters and getting their songs placed in film/TV and advertising in New York City.

Fritz LaBoucane is the Creative Director of Vidal Sassoon in Toronto.

Glenn Wiehl is a hairstylist with Elizabeth Arden at Saks Fifth Avenue in New York City.

Hedda Lettuce is a female impersonator based in New York City.

Jason Stuart is a comedian and actor from Los Angeles and had a recurring role on the TV show *My Wife and Kids*.

Kenny Bonavitacola is a fashion designer (Bill Blass, Perry Ellis, his own BONAVITACOLA label, and many more) and restaurateur in New York City.

Kevin Aviance is a performer and recording artist with #1 Billboard chart hits.

Kevin Kelly is a freelance floral designer/flower arranger from Kansas City, Missouri, and author of *Letting the Lotus Bloom: The Expression of Soul Through Flowers*.

Kevin Scott was a stylist/hair colorist at Christophe's Beverly Hills salon and recently opened C. Kevin at Absolution.

Keoni Udarbe is a pediatrician and child psychiatry private clinician in New York City.

Kyle Barton is a college student in Boston, Massachusetts.

Matthew Link is a journalist and filmmaker who has written for *Time*, *Newsweek*, and many travel publications and has produced his own guidebooks and documentaries that have played on PBS and in film festivals.

Michael Alvear is the co-host of HBO's *The Sex Inspectors* and author of the gay sex and relationship advice book *Men Are Pigs but We Love Bacon*.

Michael McDerman is a performing artist and female impersonator in New York City and is also known as Carmella Cann.

Michael Musto writes the well-known "La Dolce Musto" celebrity and gossip column in the *Village Voice* in New York City and also appears on TV commenting on entertainment stories.

Michael Thomas Ford is a writer from northern California who is best known for his "Trials of My Queer Life" series of essay collections and novels including *Last Summer* and *Looking for It*.

Michele Antiga is Technical Director, specialized in coloring but also cutting and styling, at the Daniel Hersheson Salon in Harvey Nichols in London, England, and is originally from Italy.

Mike Luongo is a New York–based freelance writer, editor, and photographer, concentrating on travel in the Middle East and

Latin America, and wrote Frommer's first edition of *Buenos Aires Guidebook.*

Patrick Sherman is a self-employed editor/journalist from San Diego, California.

Randall David Cook is a playwright/screenwriter in New York City.

Randy Dotinga earns his living as a freelance writer in San Diego.

Rick Trabucco is a comedian and interior designer in New York City.

Travis D. Bone is a reporter and columnist for a newsmagazine in San Diego, California, called *The Gay and Lesbian Times.*

Vinnie Petrarca is a partner in CP Promotions, doing special events and promotion in New York City.

Yiannis Psaroudis calls himself an aspiring comic in SoHo (New York City).

TROLLING FOR MR. RIGHT, THEN SETTLING FOR MR. NOT TOO WRONG

Why a Man as Your #1 Goal Sabotages Happiness

"Women sometimes go out of their way to find this Mr. Right, to the point where it becomes a vocation for them."

—Alex

Do you search for Mr. Right? Is each outing with friends another opportunity to scope out a potential partner? When finding a man dominates your life, you devalue yourself and compromise your happiness. The stereotype goes like this: Men are brought up believing that much of their self-worth comes from accomplishments; women are taught that theirs comes from an ability to get a man and get more points if he has an impressive career and money. So women often put most of their energy into finding and keeping a man, while men put their energy into proving how much they can achieve. A man's self-esteem increases with each career milestone, salary raise, victory over something, woman he scores with, or extra pounds he lifts in the gym. A woman's self-esteem goes down with each man who does her wrong.

"The whole world is brainwashed into believing that a woman is nothing without a man."   —Kevin S.

Making Men the Center of Your Universe

The relationship sections in bookstores teem with material on how to find and keep a man. Why do we spend so much money and time learning strategies to handle men and keep them content? Most men don't go to these lengths to keep us happy! The exception is reading sex tips so they can get more. All of this reinforces the inflated importance of men. Rick gets frustrated when he sees women put their needs aside to cater to a man's. He explains:

❝ As a designer, one of the most painful things I see is women designing their apartment like some great, big mantrap. I had a client who asked me specifically to choose furnishings for her home in which a man would feel comfortable because she was preparing her home for a man. I said, 'How about you in the meantime? What are you going to enjoy?' That didn't matter to her. It was all about somebody else. **❞**

> " 'I need a man! I need a man! I need a man!' I get so sick of my straight girlfriends saying that. I just want to slap them and say that is so gross to think you can't have a well-rounded life without a man."
> —Matthew

Men aren't prizes. Many books encourage us to try hard to hunt him down and play games to lure him in. What is the value of that prize? Staying in a role to keep the games going? Catering to him? Going along with his whims? Putting up with bad behavior? Unhappiness with some delicious crumbs thrown in? Make yourself a prize that he'll want to have! We won't tell you how to find and keep a man. Instead, we encourage you to take the emphasis off of HIM, and put it on YOU. Find yourself first—create your own happiness. Open your eyes and pay attention! The better-than-nothing guy will leave you wallowing in regrets later. Being impatient about finding a man leads to unsatisfying choices, as Patrick points out:

> ❝ Whether through social hardwiring, an unwillingness to deal with any potential fear, or uncertainty and loneliness caused by seeking out a decent and intelligent man, many well-meaning, heterosexual women continue to sell themselves short—settling into a loveless marriage and subservient homemaker mode with the first or second cretin to satisfy them sexually. Don't do it! Good things come to women who wait. ❞

"If all you want to do is make sure that a man is around you, you won't evolve or prosper. You could be very bored with your life. Be strong!"

—Kevin A.

Stop making a man the center of your universe. He can be the sweetest part of your life, but not your whole life. Men don't make us as important as we make them. Please throw out your hunting books and begin to value yourself and your life. We'll help you find your path to a more satisfying life that doesn't revolve around having a man!

Going on a Manhunt

Manhunts get serious. We use bait—short skirts, visible cleavage, sexy perfume, flirting, sex, and devious tactics toward other women—to lure a man. But once you reel him in, are you satisfied? After getting into a relationship for the sake of having one, you may complain to your friends more than you share how great he is. Alex thinks manhunts are wasted energy and suggests:

❝ It's a bad idea to spend your time looking for somebody. You are better off just going about your daily life and taking care of yourself. Eventually somebody will come along who intrigues you in a way that you'll want to go out with him. Don't go out on a limb to find somebody. Just keep your eyes open. **❞**

"When some women go on a manhunt, they bring too much ammunition and a single-minded determination that they're going to get a man no matter what, as if any old man is a prize. Do you think that anything that you can catch with a net or hook or bayonet is worth it?"   —Rick

Manhunts minimize the good aspects of your own life. There's a lot of stress involved in the search. And games. Relationships should be fun, not a nerve-racking all-out plan to lure a man by playing a role that you think will appeal to him. When you begin with games, your potential for trust and sincerity decreases. Why act like you're not good enough the way you are? Kevin S. says you sell yourself short by putting too much emphasis on satisfying his needs:

66 Look at the book of rules, telling you what to do and what not to do. You're turning away from YOUR likes and dislikes when you follow them and try to figure out how to turn yourself into a mantrap. Then you're not an honest person. Later, the egg will crack and the real person will emerge—an alien! 99

Manhunts are counterproductive. Have you ever needed a particular blouse or shoes but couldn't find them, no matter how hard you looked? Then when you don't need them, there they are. It's the same with men, explains Michael M.:

66 Women who make finding a man most important obviously haven't heard the expression, 'having it all.' A man is just one part of

having it all. There are so many other options for women nowadays other than just finding a partner. It doesn't happen when you're looking for it. Finding the right person happens in an unexpected way, or it's someone you happen to meet when you're not looking. You have to be open to it in general, but not just go on this nonstop hunt. If you make finding a man an obsessive quest, you're screwing yourself over **99**

Rushing to Find a Partner

We usually analyze each guy as a potential partner project WAY too soon. Then we're disappointed when expectations aren't met. Travis is no different. He even admits that he's gotten a little over-ambitious with his future projections about a guy:

66 My biggest problem with dating is I always put the cart before the horse, you know, just thinking stupid things like, 'Oh, if we got married what would our hyphenated names be.' I was once dating a guy whose last name was Woody, and I really didn't want the name on the joint checking account to be Bone-Woody. In all seriousness, though, the point I am trying to make is a lot of times we tend to get ahead of ourselves because we start thinking about what-ifs and what could be. **99**

Travis adds that it's even worse when you try to predict what your guy is thinking and take it a step further: second-guessing what you think he'd like or what kind of woman he'd want you to be. A false front isn't fair to him, or you. Travis cautions from experience that you should slow down and be YOU. He explains:

66 Trust me, I am guilty of this. What I have learned to do is just relax into dating and don't get ahead of yourself. As a result you end up staying calm and don't end up playing games. If you just go with the flow, you show more of yourself. That is a win/win in the end—he falls for you because of who you are and not because you are trying to be the person you think he wants, and you get to be more comfortable with yourself. 99

Do you get excited when meeting a potential partner and jump in without getting to know him well? When you get burned, do you ask, "Why can't this one be different?" Because you didn't handle it differently! Hello! If you keep diving in with a man who says what you want to hear and don't wait to know who he really is, don't blame him if he later disappoints or hurts you. Until you take yourself more seriously, men won't either. Get to know a man before deciding if you want to be involved with him. Men (and women!) hide less-attractive qualities that will come out if you're patient. Randall advises waiting to see if he's worth your time before getting involved:

66 Most men are not worth meeting. Save that energy for when you meet a man who really deserves your time and attention. Set some standards and keep them, even when things feel difficult and desperate. There's nothing worse than actually being on a bad date and feeling lonelier than you did when you were alone. 99

Dating More Like Men

When men date, they're more likely looking to have fun or hoping to get laid. With women, the mind-set is often "Is he THE ONE?" or "Will he make a good partner?" Men have more fun by dating casually and letting anything beyond that happen naturally. If you learn to do that too, you'll enjoy the process more. It takes a long time to know if someone will be a good partner. Why not enjoy getting to know a guy instead of worrying about future commitments? When you relax and enjoy life, you're seen as more attractive. Lighten up on dating! Don't make each new guy so important that you get stressed waiting for him to call and fall apart if he doesn't. David points out that women don't understand that their mental attitudes ultimately make them more attractive:

66 You can work on the outside—body check, lose some weight, put on makeup, get red hair—that's easy! But you need to change your behavior. Learn not to get crazy if HE doesn't call. Everybody has a life. Be willing to accept the fact that maybe he doesn't want to call you back. There's 31 flavors at Baskin-Robbins. You might not be the flavor he likes. It's not that there's anything wrong with you. You just weren't for him. That's it. Move on and know what you're worth. You can't look outside of yourself for that. 99

"Don't set yourself up to be his latest lay because neediness keeps you from distinguishing between sincerity and him playing into your needs."   —Kyle

Learn to date the way men do. Go out just to have fun, without projecting into the future until there's a good reason to. Turn off your crystal ball. It doesn't work! No more hunting mode! Flirt. Play. Someone might make you happy if you're not looking. It's more fun than bagging nothing in a hunt. Carl has a realist take on Mr. Right:

66 Mr. Right Now certainly exists. But I don't buy the romantic notion that there's a perfect 'one' for every person on the planet. I think what's more realistic is that there are probably any number of people who would be suitable life partners for you—if the timing is right for both of you. And people do change over time. Mr. Right today might be Mr. Wrong ten years from now. Think of this as a journey, not so much a final destination that you reach when you find Mr. Right and everything will be magical for the rest of your life. It's more fluid than that. 99

When you anxiously go looking for Mr. Right, you might as well have a siren on your head that warns guys you're on the make and they should run. Your attitude shouts that you're looking for a relationship. Men say it's a major turnoff. One who stays may take advantage of you. When that happens, you'll call him a jerk or loser, eventually end it, move on to the next one, and the pattern continues. Let us help you change that! Alex warns that it makes a very bad impression:

66 A woman who's making a big effort to find a man is unattractive. It makes men think 'What is wrong with her? Why is she just waiting for the next man to come into her life? Why is she desperate and so needy?' It definitely will put men off. 99

"People can smell desperation. Some people are attracted to that smell, but they may not be the ones you want to form a long-term relationship with."   —Dan

Living in Fantasy

Do you have a romantic notion of "Mr. Right"? Are you looking for that one perfect man? Some of us set our standards way too low. But seeking Mr. Right sets a standard that no one can live up to. Reassess what's really important in a romantic partner. When looking for someone who fills one set of needs, you can miss a guy who fulfills more important ones. Alex suggests you rethink who Mr. Right is:

66 I don't think there is a Mr. Right. I do believe there are many Mr. Wrongs. There are many people out there who fit the situation you're in right now. I think women should definitely have their standards—intelligence and personality are things to be picky about. When it comes to getting picky about more minor details, that's when they run into trouble. Women can be more open-minded about dating different sorts of people who don't necessarily fit into their ideal type without lowering their standards. 99

> "Everyone comes with baggage, and it's a matter of figuring out what's acceptable to you. To expect to find a great, untouched male is unrealistic."   —Vinnie

NO man can fill Mr. Right's shoes. There's no such thing as a perfect partner, no matter what TV, movies, and books show. Get off Fantasy Island! Drop distorted romantic images that can only be conjured up by a writer. That perfect romantic lover doesn't exist. If you actually found a man who catered to your romantic side, friends might wonder if he's gay! Accept that straight men have limits. We all want the perfect guy, including Travis. But he explains that it's more satisfying to lighten up on unrealistic expectations:

   " I am so guilty of this too. What's really awesome is when you find a guy and you see his faults and yeah, they might bug you, but in a way that makes you smile and that you think is cute. **"**

> "In real life, your dream guy may be Mr. Makes-Me-Happy-Most-of-the-Time."   —Randy

Live on Earth, not in films and books. Give men a break. It's not fair to hold them to fictitious standards. Listen to celebrity news to see how imperfect those perfect actors are in their real-life relationships—more like revolving doors than the way they are in the movies that we look to for standards. Reality dating shows have added another dimension to finding a man and being romanced off your feet. Vinnie says he's watched shows like *The Bachelor* and *The Bachelorette* and is concerned about the messages these kinds of shows give women. He explains:

66 If that's your expectations, you're bound to be disappointed. They set it up like it's real. No one wins someone on a game show! It's such a wish fulfillment. The men go along with the flowers and other gestures that women long for. P-u-l-ease! That's never going to happen in real life. Honey, that's what you have gay friends for! 99

Ultimately, the best relationship comprises two people who like each other for who they are and accept each other's glitches because they appreciate their good attributes. According to Fritz, some women set unrealistically high standards that they measure all men against while looking for Mr. Right:

66 The bar is set so unbelievably high or unrealistically that nobody alive will fit that role. If you love somebody, love them warts and all! Everyone has great qualities, but there will always be things about someone that you wish weren't there. You have to look at him and decide whether you can overlook a few shortcomings in order to benefit from all the positive things. Be willing to accept both. Many people get into a relationship, find one tiny little flaw, and obsess about it. It becomes much bigger than it is.

And they break it off with that person because of one little thing. But if you keep writing everybody off because of one flaw, you're never going to meet anyone. Look at yourself. Are you perfect? Do you have any flaws that you hope others will overlook? 🙶

"Most of our standards are unrealistic. Everyone comes with their own toolbox of plusses and minuses."   —Brian

Ah, when you're with a guy who makes you happy, find the sweetness in his quirks and learn to laugh instead of nag. Sometimes we don't even know what would truly make us happy. A guy who has lots of money, a hot-looking hunk, or one who'd make your mom proud won't necessarily rock your world. When you meet a guy who you get along with but he doesn't ace your checklist, don't be so quick to dismiss him. Bob advises giving a decent guy a chance:

🙶 It's simple enough to me. As a rule for all women, I would say, 'Go for it.' If you see someone you like, whom you respect, who treats you with intelligence and courtesy and perhaps a smile, and heck, he's not married, engaged, or wearing a ring, go for it. Don't wait for your heart to do somersaults, your G-spot to melt, or your friends to tell you he's out of your league or you're out of his. Take a chance and connect with someone who you find interesting and worthwhile. 🙶

Put qualities that make up a man's character, like integrity, sincerity, and being appreciative of you, higher on the list of what you'd like. A great relationship with a guy who has a lot of good qualities is easier to attain if you accept that you'll never find perfection. Dan advises accepting that all men will have their glitches and being open-minded about a good one with some annoying but tolerable qualities:

> ❝ If you find somebody that you really like, recognize that it might be rare and don't let silly things get in the way. Men are men, and they're wired in a certain way. There are too many expectations put on that realm. ❞

There's nothing wrong with wanting to be attracted to him too, as long as you don't seek perfection. You can't shop for a guy with the same eye as shopping for shoes. He's a person, not a product. If you end up with one jerk after another, go within to figure out why. David thinks:

> ❝ In order to have a good relationship, look at your core relationships with your parents, especially your father. What didn't you get from him? Are you going to spend the rest of your life looking for love from the next man you're with? If you didn't get that, you have to first be okay with what you did or didn't get from your father. Once you get that in order, you can seriously date others. Otherwise you pick the same type of men over and over, and it never works out. ❞

At Least He's Breathing!

"So he's not what I wanted. Do you know how few men are available?" Have you ever said that? You set high standards and searched. And searched. And searched. After going through a slew of jerks and not seeing what you'd ideally love, you may go to the other extreme by settling for anyone available, rather than be alone. Randy says he sees it often and suggests:

> ❝ If you look for a man who will meet all your needs, no one will ever measure up and you'll spend your life being disappointed. But too many women go in the exact opposite direction—they lower their expectations so far that anyone who shows them an occasional glimpse of affection seems to be the man of their dreams. Work toward keeping your expectations in the middle, and forget about finding Mr. Right unless you happen to be Ms. Right. ❞

Someone is NOT better than no one! Settling won't bring happiness. You get a quick fix of having a partner, pleasing Mom, and showing you can get someone. If you marry a guy who's just better than nothing, don't expect to be happy after you've had your dream wedding day, explains Kevin K.:

> ❝ I have personally found that settling leads to joyless involvement and frustration at closing off the opportunity for relationships that would come with joy and enthusiasm. I decided the real task was not to try to appease the unhappy half but rather to increase

the happiness quotient. The sad thing about settling is it takes away that opportunity, because it takes so much energy just to survive. If a woman is settling, she needs to step back and do real soul searching. **"**

People push us to find a man, especially moms, who also get pressured. "Why doesn't your daughter have a boyfriend? It's time to be a grandma." Unhappy women push others to grab up some available straight man. They don't learn from experience! Michael M. explains:

" If you settle, you don't think you deserve the best. You just think you deserve something. You're so afraid of being alone, afraid of your own thoughts and feelings, that you think you have to hook up with someone. It's a sad commentary. Settling for a man is like saying you're going to the store for a dress and they don't have dresses but they have slips. You're not going to wear a slip to work every day. That's absurd. Settling sells your own ass down the river. **"**

"If you settle to have a guy, it's probably going to be someone you don't want to be with. That's like the movie fantasy—it's not going to happen."   **—Vinnie**

Don't just take what you can get to appease others. Step back and honestly ask yourself if he's really someone you want to be with. Your happiness is at stake when you buy into other people's values, even if people bug you to settle. Get earplugs if necessary! There are lots of guys who can make you happy without going to extremes. Look to real-life couples instead of fictional ones as role models for what you want. Carl advises getting a balance of the most important qualities combined with tolerance for those that aren't as desirable. He says:

> 66 Forget everything you've seen in those Lifetime movies at two in the morning. . . . The fairy-book romance may happen for B-movie actresses, but it ain't happening for most normal people. You should be seeking an equal partner who respects you and never disrespects you. There will be good times and bad, but the goal is to have more good and to feel like you're both true partners who can count on each other no matter what life throws your way. 99

Men consistently say that they don't like being pursued by women who are obviously searching for a partner. They can tell by the questions you ask and the way you talk about your own life that you're sizing him up with an eye to the future. Most prefer a woman who seems enthusiastic about her life. When you control your needs and date for fun, a man is more likely to stick around. Acting like you strongly need him can motivate a hit-and-run—he takes advantage and then disappears. David implores:

> 66 Don't settle for what you don't want. You need to raise your standards. Nothing is worse than being desperate. People can smell it. Nobody likes it. It's not attractive. In the beginning it's nice to have somebody need you, but it always turns around and slaps you in the face. Always! 99

Make Yourself Happy First

If you create a happy life that doesn't depend on having a man, you won't settle for one whose best quality is being available. Redefine your version of happiness! *Not miserable* doesn't mean happy. Look in any thesaurus for synonyms for *happiness*. You'll never see "having a man" or "not being alone" or "being able to prove that someone wants you." Spend some time reflecting, advises Kevin S.:

> **❝** What makes you happy? Stop listening to your girlfriends and the magazines telling you what to do and wear. Being unhappy is miserable. You turn your angst and hatred of yourself into full force and direct it to the outside world. Who wants to be around when you're miserable? It segregates you more and more from everything that's going on. Who wants to hang out with Mopey? **❞**

"Ask yourself really strong questions. What do I feel I'm lacking? Why am I looking to a man to fill those needs?"   —David

We'll remind you throughout this book that happiness comes from inside you. Too many women forget what being happy actually feels like in their pursuit of a man. There's a big difference between feeling safe and feeling happy. Waking up smiling after a good night's sleep is much more pleasant than obsessing over HIM and waking up feeling unsettled. Manhunts minimize the good aspects of your life and prevent you from developing a happy one on your own. Leave being a hound for real dogs. Yiannis recommends respecting your life enough to wait for a healthy partner, explaining:

66 Like the soap opera says, you only got one life to live. Are you going to spend it settling or searching? The right guy is out there, and even if it takes fifteen years to find him, I'd rather spend fifteen years with Mr. Right than thirty years with Mr. Oh-Hell-What-Was-I-Thinking? 99

"Here in New York my clients complain they can't meet the right guy. I tell them to leave themselves open to adventure. Don't settle. Be comfortable being by yourself."   **—Glenn**

First-Aid Tips

- If you don't have friends with positive attitudes and who are fun to be with, find new ones, and spend time with them.
- Try something that you've always wanted to do but had no time for it (if you stop trolling for men that day, there's more time).
- Declare men off-limits for a week and focus on yourself. Don't discuss men with friends, read romance novels, or consider them when making plans.
- Buy a vibrator.

COMPLETE YOURSELF!

Revising a Man's Place in Your Life

"Cameron Crowe should be spanked for this 'completion' business. Jerry Maguire is major fiction. Each one of us is complete; we are not a half of a whole. To think so begs for expensive psychotherapy."

—Randall

Were you taught to make finding and keeping a man THE important component in your life? Do you feel like nothing without one? This must change if you want to be happy and attract a healthy man. Making a man your whole life is dangerous! It forces you to put up with unacceptable behavior to avoid not being alone and keeps you on edge if you worry about losing him.

When you make a man your life, you lose yourself in the process—which sets you up to get no more than the bits of happiness HE throws at you. It's time to stop looking for a man to complete you! No one can complete you but you, no matter what the media or your mother tells you.

Which Half Are You?

Were you taught to make satisfying a man's needs your prime responsibility—to keep him happy so he'll stay? It's time to rethink that position for your own good! Putting most of your energy into HIM makes getting your own needs met optional. Stereotypes don't have to be your reality. Curt suggests leaving behind roles that you may have been taught or exposed to:

" Find out who you are and become yourself, not what you've been taught. Work toward gaining strength and security. Break stereotypes about women. You mustn't think you're weaker than a man is—that energy can distract you from what you really want to accomplish. "

If you lose yourself in someone else, your happiness is dependent on him, so you lose control over it. Developing yourself as a whole person gives you power to leave a man who isn't good for you and not let in another poor choice. Rick believes you devalue your worth when you define yourself by a man. He says:

" Whether you're a man or woman, if your whole existence is based around being with somebody, you are truly devaluing yourself—you can't make someone else more important than you. I think that you're suffering from a very skewed value system. You have to view yourself as the prize. When you do, they come to you. "

Do you have a misconception that you should be half in a relationship? Which half? The one that does all the work or who puts up with unfair behavior from the other half? Two halves do not make a healthy whole in a relationship. Both partners should be whole on their own. As Alex explains:

> " A woman who says that she needs a man to complete her has her math all wrong. She believes that in a relationship two halves come together to make a whole. But what happens when the relationship dissolves? That woman is then only half a person. However, a woman who finds fulfillment in herself is a complete person, and a much better partner. One and one should equal one healthy relationship. "

Do you use "we think" when you're in a relationship? That often means what HE thinks. Many women adopt their guy's preferences and opinions to please HIM. When you feel complete on your own, you have a real identity. Concentrate more on completing yourself than on finding a man to do it for you, adds Yiannis:

> " If you rely on a man to complete you, you're dependent upon him to make you whole. What happens when he's gone? Besides, if you're looking to him to complete you, that means that you're bringing less than a whole person to the party, and how fair is that to him? "

Needing a guy as your other half motivates you to sacrifice your own preferences and adopt his. No wonder men are spoiled! If you

always give him his way, why shouldn't he enjoy the ride? It's up
to you to stop the pattern. Working on yourself allows you to steer.
Curt explains:

> 66 Women who look for inner strength in someone else are
> looking to that person for fulfillment. I think a woman should feel
> secure with herself before she brings someone else into her life.
> You have to have a strong foundation. 99

Completing yourself helps you to be an equal partner in a relationship. Needing a guy to complete you keeps you stuck in the
revolving door of getting involved with one man after another who
is unhealthy or disrespectful. Michael McD. says that you can
change that pattern:

> 66 A man is never going to complete you. If you think so, you
> need self-work, and that means you'll always be jumping from
> relationship to relationship to find someone to complete you. 99

Know thyself! Throughout the book the guys will encourage
you to work on developing yourself as a content woman and provide suggestions for increasing your happiness. When you focus
on doing things that you love instead of making his needs yours,
you'll smile more. Happiness on the inside gives you more confidence and keeps you stronger when a cute jerk is trying to bait
you. That's the best way to find a healthy, satisfying relationship.
A happy girl doesn't need a man to give her a life. When you learn

to appreciate yourself, you won't want to be half of anything, and, as Alex notes, you'll accept and expect as much good as you give:

> ❝ You shouldn't build your life around anyone. You need to be complete in yourself so you can contribute to the relationship. Compromise is definitely part of a relationship, but not to the point that one is giving more than the other. When I say 'compromise,' I mean reaching an agreement and being partners in a relationship, not compromising your integrity. Until you start seeing yourself as equal to men, you'll be less in the relationship. Both partners should be able to take equally from it. ❞

"You have to know who you are before you can expect to find someone to love. Of course, only gay men take the time to do that. Straight men are 'I don't have the time for that touchy feely stuff'—outside the bedroom." —Ed

The Myth of "You Complete Me"

"You complete me" sounds romantic, but that's momentary. It worked in *Jerry Maguire,* but real life is another story. In movies the girl gets the guy in a perfect way. We strive for a fairy tale–like romance but often get someone who turns into a frog. Frogs and jerks and even very nice guys who do treat you well can't complete you. Nobody can complete you but YOU! Michael A. agrees:

66 There's a tremendous amount of pressure for women to settle because of an idea that there's something wrong with her if a man does not complete her, as if she were some kind of jigsaw puzzle in which the last piece is being hidden from her. Or that she's too stupid, or not good-looking enough or trying hard enough to find that last missing piece. 99

"If you come from the point of view that 'I am this incomplete person unless I have you'—what a burden to put on another human being. Period! Men don't like that burden. Nobody would."
—Matthew

Thinking in terms of a man completing you leaves you feeling much less than whole without one. A man may fill a void that you believe you can't fill yourself. But that doesn't mean that you'll be any more complete with a partner if you don't complete yourself first. Travis has a much better perspective:

66 You need someone who complements you. I know all of these guys (big pet peeve here) who say I am looking for someone like me, and I think to myself, 'Are you nuts?' I could never date someone like me; I'd drive myself nuts. I want a guy who isn't like me but is interested in what I have to offer a relationship, and likewise, someone who has skills, talents, or experiences that are enriching for me. 99

Complement is a good operative word. A partner who may not understand you but gives support anyway and who has interests you can share, and vice versa, is one who adds to your life instead of giving you one. When you complement each other, Keoni says you become a good team instead of one half trying to fit with another:

> 66 Synergy is created by two people bringing their skills and talents together. The old adage that behind every good man is a good or better woman is true. In today's environment, couples can be powerful teams, and the most impartment element is the independence and strength brought by each person. 99

A couple who complement each other share their strengths. You may be more outgoing and energetic and help him to network while he helps you calm down. Or his creative passions may loosen you up a bit. When you each bring different strengths into a relationship, you can learn from each other and grow together, Plus, it's more interesting to be with someone who doesn't think and act exactly like you! Michael T.F. says having a healthy relationship begins with becoming healthy on your own:

> 66 Relationships are about sharing, and in order for any relationship to be successful you have to already have a life you love to share with this other person. Concentrate on making your life as rich and full as it can possibly be, and THEN think about finding someone to share it with. 99

What does *complete* mean to you? Settling for a man to be dependent on? Catering to him so he won't leave? Accepting a life that doesn't generate consistent happiness? Does that make sense? Carl advises dropping the "You complete me" expectation:

66 When was the last time you saw a man complete anything?? Remember that shelving he promised to install in the basement? Here's a tip: You can't rely on ANYONE else to make your life complete—not your friends, not your family, and certainly not your boyfriend. In the final analysis, we're all responsible for our own happiness, so work on making yourself happy first. If you're not satisfied with your life to begin with, a relationship isn't a magic elixir that will solve all your problems. 99

"There is nothing more attractive than a woman who exudes independence, while showing vulnerability and leaving some space for a man to fit."
                                                                —Kenny

Get this through your head because it will never change: The only way to be complete is to complete yourself. Get help if you can't free yourself without it. Sometimes a good therapist can help you work more effectively on your insecurities to enable you to strengthen your inner self-image and make you feel like a whole person on your own. When you can get past blocks that reinforce a man's importance to your happiness, you can learn to be whole on your own. Healthy independence is an awesome quality! Alex advises taking a stand against old stereotypes:

66 The only way the vicious cycle of pressure will stop is if women stand up and say 'I don't need someone to complete me. I can complete myself.' If someone comes along, and someone will come along if you're a already a complete person—because that's attractive—then there's much more you can give to the relationship because you're not this half trying to find another half. 99

Stand up now and say "I don't need someone to complete me. I can complete myself!" Invite some girlfriends over and do it together as a group activity. Reinforce each other as you break old stereotypes. If you say it enough, you might just believe it one day. Once you think it, the next step is feeling it. You've been brainwashed into making men overly important—now brainwash yourself. The more you say it, the more it will sink in. "I don't need someone to complete me. I can complete myself!" Put yourself into a win/win situation and enjoy the power it gives you. It's also more attractive to a healthy man, as Matthew explains:

66 Men want to have an equal partner. You have a different set of strengths, but men on some level understand what those strengths are. Men want someone who can stand her ground and be a partner with him. Women who come at it from an unequal, dependent point of view exude 'I'm less than you are.' It's wrong on so many levels. 99

Man = Cheesecake

Do you have a seriously fattening food that you love, like cheesecake? Have you ordered it in a restaurant you've never tried and been disappointed? It's frustrating to eat tons of calories you don't need and not get the pleasure you'd hoped for. It's similar with men. Why give up time to please a guy if he doesn't please you back? A man can be a delicious part of your life. But he shouldn't be your life. That's your responsibility. Once you're complete, you can support each other. Says David:

66 You need to be independent/interdependent—being with somebody because you want to be with them, not because you HAVE TO be with them. The hardest thing we have to learn is to love ourselves first, in every way—mentally, emotionally, spiritually, and physically. Be the best YOU that you can be. 99

"Having a man is like owning a pair of Manolo Blahniks. They are both fabulous to have if you can find the right ones, but you don't really need them to be happy."   —Kyle

Have you ever been tempted by a dessert you wanted but chose to pass because you didn't need cake to feel satisfied after dinner? There's a BIG difference between needing and wanting—cheesecake or a man. Needing makes you ignore calories, or aggravation, even if there's little pleasure. Wanting helps you be selective and wait for the yummy cheesecake or healthy man. When your life is very satisfying, only a delicious guy will be worth the calories of your time. I appreciate good cheesecake when I find it. And I WANT a tasty man, very much. But my happiness doesn't depend on it, so I can be choosy. I taste test—get to know him—slowly, and enjoy the time we're not together too. Alex warns for your own well-being:

66 It's important to find yourself first and do what you have to. Then it doesn't feel like you'll spontaneously combust by a certain date if you don't find a man. 99

When you make men your cheesecake instead of your life, it's a win/win relationship. Create a life that you enjoy (more in Chapter 9). You can't go out with every guy you're attracted to, but you CAN control who you pass on. Choose dessert wisely!

Me, Myself, & I

Are you a wimp about being on your own? "What will I do?" is a common response from women when their guy wants to see friends or do something alone. Many of us weren't encouraged to develop interests or activities that we love, explains Mike:

66 We all need a life outside of our love. A friend of mine once said she melted into her love's life, becoming a part of him. It's beautiful and poetic to say it, but can be damaging if overdone. 99

"A woman should be able to do anything a man can. No woman is an island, but every once in a while she should be comfortable being like one."   —Alex

Growing up, our interactions often revolved around finding a boyfriend—primping and planning strategies—while guys played ball, horsed around, and got drunk. So we often don't associate getting together with friends as the kind of fun that guys do. But you can learn to have more pleasure with your girlfriends, and solo too (which I discuss more in Chapter 9). Learn the "A" word—AUTONOMY—to relish your own company and function and thrive on your own. An autonomous woman has better things to do than put up with a guy who isn't satisfying or who doesn't treat her well. The healthiest relationship is one in which each person maintains his and her autonomy. Rick adds:

66 You cannot be in a healthy relationship with anyone else if you aren't in one with yourself. To have autonomy and be able to be with yourself is a huge gift. It's really throwing something away if you can't do it. 99

"Independence allows you to shed your desperation and write your own story line, using imagination inspired by a fantasy that, like fragrance from incense, comes from knowing yourself."

—Kevin K.

If you and your partner can both handle your own needs, you're together because you want to support each other, not because you can't do without a partner. It's fun to do things apart and share experiences. Couples that maintain separate friends and interests tend to appreciate their time together more because they have time to miss each other. Neither feels dependent nor completely depended on, so the tone of the relationship is free yet committed. Keoni explains that really being complete means having autonomy:

66 The most attractive, capable men prefer a companion instead of an escort. While there is synergy in couples that may feel more whole or complete, it is an illusion to believe I am not a whole person without another to validate or direct my life. Besides, I never wanted to date half of anything, man or woman. 99

Few couples like all of the same things. Why not indulge your interests? Why drag him to the theater if he hates it or schlep to a ballgame when you don't enjoy it? Have a girl's night out. Or try a weekend at a spa or doing activities with friends. Then come home, share experiences, and jump each other's bones. When you each have a whole life, the time you spend together is a choice, not an obligation. Travis has observed that couples who maintain autonomy are stronger:

66 Hands down, the healthiest couples I know do things apart and have their own interests and separate friends. Of course you want to have things that both of you enjoy doing together, but

girls, come on. You don't need to follow your guy out to the golf course and ride around in the little cart with him all day just to spend time with him if you don't like it. Let him go do his thing; you can do dinner afterward or something else. Everyone needs their own 'me time.' 🙶🙶

"Ironically, if you have no sense of being alone, you often end up alone. Men will avoid you."   —Rick

Autonomy is a delightful gift you can give to yourself. When your guy wants to go out with his friends, surprise him by NOT asking "What will I do?" Plan to do something you're happy to have time for. When you're in a relationship and he's busy, relish the time to make your own plans instead of dreading it. Michele explains that creating space nurtures intimacy:

🙶🙶 We all need our space. It makes you feel alive, independent, stronger, and helps you enjoy your time together more because you miss each other and refresh passion and fantasies. 🙶🙶

Do you worry that men won't be comfortable with your independence? Many aren't, but that's their problem. Men are turned on by a woman who can take care of herself. But just as cultural stereotypes teach us we need a man to feel complete, men are taught they need to take care of women. Many get scared of one who's in control of herself since he doesn't feel needed to take care of her.

She can also control her need for him and is more likely to walk if he pulls too much nonsense. Independence threatens men who need to feel in control. But you MUST be true to you. Don't play a role to please HIM. Reassure him that he's still needed in many ways. Support from a caring partner is a delight. And don't go to the other extreme by making him feel he's not needed at all. We all need support. Michael McD. recommends finding a balanced independence:

> **❝** Guys like independent women because it takes some pressure off them. But a guy still likes to feel to some extent like he's 'the man' in the relationship. While you can be independent, don't take it to the point where you feel like the man in the relationship. That can hurt his ego. Everyone has an ego to protect. As long as you're independent in the sense of being able to do things for yourself, it's fine—but not to the point of not letting anyone in close. Don't feel you have to be completely independent. That doesn't exist. That means you're not allowing yourself to be vulnerable and you have a trust issue with men—a self-protective thing. **❞**

An independent woman can attract yet at the same time intimidate guys who need to feel needed. Develop what I call comfortable independence—knowing that you can take care of yourself, while being able to accept support from a man you trust. Don't go overboard trying to prove independence. When you know who you are, it can be a subtle presence that you live by, not announce. For instance, Hedda suggests:

> ❝ Always have your own money, your own friends outside of his, and your own apartment. Sleep in his as often as you like—stay there all the time if you want. But when you need your space to be alone, you can always pop over to your place, light some candles, slip into a bubble bath, and listen to your Norah Jones CD. ❞

Healthy men do find autonomy attractive and can handle a woman who's her own person. Develop your autonomy slowly. Think about what you like, and how often you didn't express your preferences in order to go along with HIS. Having your own mind, and expressing it, is a big shot of self-esteem. When you accept that you can complete yourself, your power begins. Dan has seen this work firsthand:

> ❝ The women whom I've become closest with are people who enjoy romance but whose happiness doesn't depend on it. Everybody is under pressure from family and society to have this one relationship that works and makes their life worthwhile forever, but if anything happens to it they feel shattered, degraded, and derailed. The way that the world has evolved, there are too many things that can affect that. The women I know who are most happy are in longtime marriages, but their relationships enhance their lives, not make or break it. ❞

First-Aid Tips

- Do an activity solo that you've never done before.
- Smile at yourself in the mirror and say, "I love you," even if you don't feel it. Practice makes perfect!
- List things that you enjoy and that contribute to your happiness, that don't have to involve a man.
- Buy extra batteries for your vibrator.

STOP JERKS IN THEIR TRACKS!

Learning to Set Boundaries
for Inappropriate Behavior

*"We contribute to men being jerks by
taking a second date and not speaking up."*
—Kevin S.

It's time to stop complaining and do something about what bothers you. I often hear women whine "Why did he take advantage of me when I gave him everything?" Wake up! Men can't take advantage if you don't allow them to. In this chapter, the guys enlighten you on the difference between a real jerk and those we create. Yes, create! It's human nature to get away with what you can. If you don't stop men from doing hurtful things, YOU let it happen. If you refuse to allow your guy's unacceptable behavior, he'll either clean up his act or find another woman to abuse. It's that simple, says Kyle:

66 You CANNOT say one thing and then do another. The most common mistake that my girlfriends are guilty of is they allow boyfriends to hurt them. Men neglect them and are careless toward their emotions. They fight with their boyfriends and say

they won't put up with the bullshit anymore. But two days later she is back with the guy. After this happens a few times, the guy has the message that his jerky behavior is not only something he can get away with but that his girlfriend thinks it's acceptable. Girls, mean what you say! If you tell him you're going to leave if he cancels plans one more time, do it! If you don't stick to your word, then he'll take it as you telling him you don't really mean it. If you mean what you say, the jerky behavior will stop. 99

"Some men are not who you think they are. As my best friend says, 'Some do, some don't, who cares why, NEXT!' If his habits bother you and he likes them, either adapt or move on." —Keoni

It's up to YOU to stop hurtful and unfair patterns by not putting up with them—from the get-go. If you initially tolerate intolerable behavior, cater to his needs while he ignores yours, accept flowers and apologies in exchange for unacceptable actions, it's time to look in the mirror and ask who the real jerk is. Ignoring warning signs that a guy may not be healthy for you keeps you in the unhappy cycle: You complain, he calms you with excuses and compliments—you forgive, relax, and he hurts you again. That continues until you face that he will never stop unless you make him with consistent boundaries.

Don't blame men for everything that makes you unhappy. You have the power to change it. The guys and I will help you develop your resolve and determination to break the cycle. Matthew wants you to understand:

" You actually have a lot more power over men than you realize and are a very powerful commodity that men need. Obviously, sexually. But men need women more than you realize, or even more than men realize or tell you. Men may not seem like it or talk that way, or even realize it consciously, but they need women a lot more than anything. If you could see yourself as a valuable need, you'd feel your power more. "

When the Man of Your Dreams Gives You Nightmares

"I don't believe in giving people a taste of their own. It's just childish and stooping. People have done that to me, and I think they're just being horrible. It's best to be forthright."   —Michael M.

Both sexes have good behavior at first and ignore annoying stuff to make a good impression. As things get more serious, things change. Women complain about attentive, seemingly perfect men who turn into cold, uncaring aliens without warning. How can you know who the real person is at the beginning? You can't. It takes time to know who someone really is and if he can be trusted to keep his word.

Yet men say what we want to hear, and we call our friends to gush about what he said and get encouraged to keep him at all costs. We try hard to please him, based on what he says, without waiting to see if his actions actually make his words true. And when he doesn't follow through, we're devastated—again. Empty promises leave us feeling empty and wondering why he gave us bull instead of the goods. You can break the cycle! According to Kevin S., the warning signs are always there, but women don't see them or choose not to see them if they believe they need the guy:

66 You don't want to see them, especially if you feel desperate. But you have to! It's not a list of warning signs, but more a distinction between proper or improper behavior. For example, sometimes you want to be smothered with love and attention, but there can be too much of that too. If it's engulfing, then you're a possession to him. Where will it go from there? It's going to get sour. You're passive at the beginning, and it feels good. You love how he's so manly and makes decisions. Did he make all of them? Did you disagree with any of them? Did you want to say something about what you were doing but couldn't? Giving up your power and missing the huge red flags keep men acting like jerks. 99

Our expectations bloom like flowers when men use words like fertilizer to feed them. But expectations often don't bloom with joy and satisfaction. It hurts when his words turn out to be real manure. Then we label him a clone of jerks before him.

"If he's late, leave without him or send him away. There's no excuse for being late or having bad manners."   —Andy

If you like playing a victim, keep jumping in with your eyes closed when he initially tastes sweet, and keep getting hurt over and over when he turns sour. If you're sick of it, take responsibility. You CAN protect yourself. Telling him you won't take it anymore but continuing to take it won't stop him. Vinnie agrees:

66 I think we're all responsible for the way people treat us. We've all been in relationships where we've said, 'He shouldn't treat me this way. That's terrible.' But we put up with it. Instead, you should say, 'Don't treat me like that.' But that's something that we have to learn to say and mean. It's hard to stand up for yourself like that, especially for women. 99

Firmly letting him know what you consider unacceptable behavior and stepping back, or out, if it continues, tells him you mean business. I know it's hard to take a stand when you've been taught to be agreeable. Tradition expects women to please and take care of everyone. It's lousy to feel like you can't let anyone down or that you'll be labeled a bitch or aggressive for taking a stand that's normal for men to do. But if you hold your ground and don't get nasty, you can set boundaries that get better results than empty threats and nagging. Michael McD. puts it into perspective:

" Women try to please men for their own need—to take care of someone. There's a caretaker personality in women due to the buildup from society—women are supposed to take care of their families and men's needs. Also, guys are used to being taken care of. It can become a co-dependency thing when you start taking care of someone else and stop taking care of yourself. Women can now decide who they are in relation to that. You can compromise on taking care of each other. But don't fall into a cycle where your own needs don't get met. Then you begin to feel you're not getting in return what you're putting out. **"**

Add "Follow Through" to Your Action Vocabulary!

If you threaten him but don't follow through, he'll just laugh and take advantage more. Mean what you say and see if he does what he says. We get into trouble by not waiting for guys to follow through on promises used to hook us. Does he describe many nice things he plans to do for you? Do they materialize, or is it just words? Stop hoping he'll fulfill those romantic dreams as you trust too quickly and don't take time to know who he really is before giving your trust and catering to him. Some women cook, clean, loan money, and accept his demands, after only knowing him a few months, or weeks or even days. And we call men jerks?! Alex believes women enable men to be jerks:

66 Men become jerks because you allow them to. That sounds simple, but it's always jerks we can't get rid of because they're so charming. It's the guy who doesn't necessarily want to commit that seems like the harder catch. The sensitive guy, who's willing to commit and start a family, is sometimes not the guy many girls want. They want the bad guys. And you know what? When you want bad guys, that's exactly what you get. You allow these jerks to stay in your life when you should work up the balls to dump them. 99

"Men will say anything to get into a woman's pants. They'll lie, do anything. They really do." —Brian

I once advised a woman on a TV talk show to leave her guy. She vehemently defended him, saying that except for lying and cheating, he was perfect. Hello! This woman moaned about how much he'd hurt her. But when I said dumping him was the obvious action to take, she rattled off how great he was in other areas. The host of the show almost fell over. I explained that when men do hurtful things, they must have redeeming qualities or no one would stay with them. Think about it. Usually men who hurt women also know how to make them feel good with compliments, romance, gifts, great sex, and so on. Don't succumb when you know how bad his other side is! Mike advises:

66 Don't let yourself fall into an abusive pattern or make excuses for his bad behavior. It's not your fault either. If he doesn't

treat you well, call him on it, and if he doesn't change, you must leave no matter how painful it might seem in the moment."

When we meet a guy with the potential for a relationship, we relinquish responsibility for his actions by ignoring or making excuses for warning signs. "I know he hurts me, but he does this or that to make me happy." His goodies don't make bad behavior acceptable! Kevin S. urges you to pay attention to ALL of his behavior:

> **"** If you're in touch with yourself at all, you have to have little ouches along the way about what isn't right. Say NO! Even if you can't figure it out in the moment, you can't tell me that later, while lying in bed, something isn't bothering you. That means you missed a red flag. Listen to how he phrases things. Is it all about what HE wants? **"**

Many men know how to play us. And why not, if we let them? Have you jumped in quickly with someone delicious when he said the "right" things? Take responsibility for creating jerks! If you allow them to get away with unacceptable behavior, you'll keep dating jerks. Pay attention to warning signs instead of ignoring what you don't like. Then you can change the situation by speaking up. Acting sweet while you stew inside isn't being straight with him, or with yourself, as Kyle has observed:

  ❝ I have friends who only end up dating someone for a few weeks, because they ignore the warning signs of a bad relationship and aren't honest with their partners about who they are and what they want. Without honesty, not only to your partner but also to yourself, a relationship will never last. **❞**

What will you lose if he leaves after you stand up to him for not treating your feelings with respect? Unhappiness? Opportunities to complain? Be prepared to see him less or cut him loose when you warn him. Disrespectful men will continue their bad behavior if you're scared of losing them and they know it. You MUST speak up if he speaks to you or behaves improperly! Silence gives him permission to continue. Opening your mouth tells him permission is over.

> "Is he disrespecting you? Repeat after me—'Buh-Bye!'"   —Ed

Identifying the Losers

While men will take advantage if you allow them to, many have the potential to make you happy. But there are men who just aren't nice. Experienced manipulators often seem perfect. They know exactly what to say and do to warm our souls into putty. They're pros at playing into our needs and use romantic/complimentary words to lower our guards, which turns sense to mush. Then they take advantage. Watch his actions. Matthew says:

66 If a man is too eager when you first meet him, that's a red flag. Women never see that. You may think, 'Oh my God, he's so into me! He keeps calling.' But that guy's a freak! It sounds horrible, but it's true. There's a difference between a guy liking you and over-liking you. Your instinct needs to tell you what makes sense and what doesn't, no matter how much you like the attention. 99

Most excessive behavior isn't healthy. When a guy courts you at full speed, it can indicate that you're fulfilling a strong need he has that makes him get carried away for a short time. But just as you're getting ecstatic, a guy often feels out of control, scares himself, and bolts—with the same energy used to dive in. Don't get caught up in his whirlwind dating. Insist on taking your time to get to know him. If he can't stop himself, be extra careful. Riding with a guy like that is heading for a crash. Being vigilant from the beginning prevents relationship accidents later on. Mike suggests you watch for contradictions in his behavior:

66 Is this too good to be true? Does he get angry and then strangely apologetic? That is a VERY bad sign. Are there things that don't seem to connect about his past? Listen, look, learn. 99

Manipulators know how to turn it on, just when you're ready to leave. Try not to fall for his Band-Aid ploys. A sweet dose of romance shouldn't make up for behavior that hurt you! Pay attention to red flags with an open mind, such as when he doesn't show up or keep his word or he talks down to you when angry. And beware of men who always expect their way. Rick explains:

66 Watch out for guys who want to make all the decisions. There's a big difference between a man who wants to show you a good time, bring you to nice places, and who also includes you in making decisions about things and one who only brings you to places that interest HIM and acts like he's taking you under his wing. Any behavior that indicates that he's going to show you around and rescue you is a red flag. 99

"When a guy blames his bad actions on you, it's a sign he's a jerk." —Vinnie

Men sometimes try to control by using the guise of taking care of you. A controlling man will try to convince you that he's looking out for your best interests and doing what he considers right for you. This control may appear to come from a place of concern and caring, but it's really him taking over everything in his own way. Carefully observe his actions and attitude toward you. Is he inconsiderate or disrespectful? Does he lie? Is it always his way, even when you ask for yours? Does he cheat or talk down to you? Be careful! He may have seen his dad disrespect his mom. Or he's been too spoiled by women to give up his way. Dan warns:

66 A lot of people get into relationships, even bad ones, because they're used to them. They feel there's a certain role they need to play, and it's often not a healthy one. People will get away with whatever you let them get away with. If the tone is set

from the start about what you'll tolerate and what you won't, then you can't get played because you won't allow it. It needs to be set from the beginning. **99**

Look for signs, such as putting you on the defensive if you speak up or twisting your words. Watch out if he insists that he knows what's best for you as he nixes your preferences and tells you what to do. A manipulator doesn't care if you're happy. He only cares about what he can get from you. Tread carefully when your gut warns you. Don't wait until he's hurt you badly, says Kevin S.:

66 You have to be honest about how you're treated. You can't be so desperate that you let things go by and intend to fix him later. In that case, you'd better be good at fixing. How many years will it take? Aren't you worth having someone who has it together now? **99**

"We cut men so much more slack in terms of good behavior, what's acceptable and how they treat other people. Not to mention all the physical stuff. It's still a man's world."   —Vinnie

Communicate what you want from the beginning. Don't ignore stuff that will bother you later. If you make the same complaints over and over to friends, do something about it. Let him know what he's done and why it bothers you. Nicely! He'll listen more objectively if you just tell him what you'd like in a friendly way instead of using a tone that indicates criticism or anger. Then be aware of the tactics men use to get away with bad behavior so you can take action if it continues, advises Vinnie:

66 Men are manipulative. We learn that from our parents. He doesn't show up on time, so he brings flowers and you make up. That's something we learn from movies. If he doesn't show up, the grown-up thing is to say that it was disrespectful. Talk in a respectful, nonthreatening way. 99

"Tell him 'When you did X, I didn't feel good about it. I didn't tell you at that moment, but my bad feeling has not gone away.'"

—Kevin S.

Take Responsibility for How Men Treat You

Have you bent over to meet a guy's needs or allowed a guy to have his way? Many men get spoiled in childhood by Mommy, and we pick up the lead as adults. Do you settle for just a little from him, especially at the beginning? Give your needs priority instead of catering to a man's with less regard for your own desires. Many potential jerks can learn to be good partners if your actions send a message about what you will and won't accept. It's your choice to allow men to treat you in ways you don't like, explains Fritz:

66 Don't accept bad treatment. Things don't happen to you. You let people do things to you, to a degree. Depending on how

you react to his behavior, the behavior will either continue, because you allowed it to, or it won't ever happen again, because you put your foot down. 🙸

"Men don't always care about how to treat you. You teach them how. They have no other indicator, so unless you're clear about how you expect and deserve to be treated, no one's going to treat you that way."   —Rick

Men will take when it's handed on the ol' silver platter. But they're more attracted to a woman who values herself, because the confidence it gives off is sexy. When you don't get on the platter, he'll work harder to please instead of just taking from you. Andy emphasizes that neither sex likes a doormat. A woman who likes herself is much more appealing than one who needs constant reassurance and asks those "Do I look fat?" types of questions that drive guys crazy. Everyone is drawn to people with good self-esteem. Yet some women go far in the other direction and become so submissive that they abdicate their power to a man. Be careful not to make yourself a prisoner of your own insecurities in a relationship, warns Michael M.:

🙸 Some of the most famous women in history have become practically like slaves to powerful men, especially in pop music, like Ronnie and Phil Spector, Ike and Tina Turner. There's a whole pattern of a Svengali and Trilby, where the guy becomes too controlling and possessive. But they all broke out. I advise that if you see it in the beginning, nip it in the bud. Either get out or make sure the situation changes. Nobody should be someone's indentured servant. 99

Some call it being nice, but sacrificing your needs isn't nice or attractive. That's the same dynamic that makes us run to bad boys. But just as there are plenty of considerate guys who aren't doormats, you can be a nice person without attracting footprints if you stop allowing people to step on you. Find a good balance between being nice and being in control of exuding a good image, advises Michael M.:

66 You have to be a nice person deep down. I'm somebody that people think is a tacky, vicious columnist, but I'm basically a nice guy from Brooklyn under the many layers. A woman should be a nice person deep down. On the surface, though, nice is boring. You have to be a little flashy and exciting or you're boring, especially in a big city. 99

"Men play women because they can! They recognize insecurity and take advantage if you let them."　　　　—Glenn

While some men use doormats for a while, few stay. Doormats are too much responsibility. Even if a guy likes you, it's scary to worry about hurting a woman who seems vulnerable. Men will bail rather than risk hurting someone who overdoes the giving. Most people don't want to feel obligated to reciprocate an overabundance of kindness. Plus, making someone else more important screams low self-esteem, which ain't attractive, ladies! You can change the dynamic if you choose to. Repeat after me—"No one can do bad things to me if I don't allow it!" So stop allowing it!

> "Not everything is your responsibility! My mother used to say to me as a kid, 'Why doesn't your father ever help me?' And I used to think, 'Help you? Why is it your job?'"   —Jason

You can't change a man's issues, but you can change your response to the behavior they cause. That can get you more of what you want. But sometimes you must walk away from him if he's too hardheaded or doesn't like you enough to adjust his attitude and bad behavior. Many factors contribute to men behaving badly, though there are some very common patterns, according to Alex:

> **"** I've met many men who are jerks. They each have their own thing. I think the biggest ones are those who are afraid—either of commitment or closeness in the relationship. Many are afraid of getting hurt if they like you too much. For some reason we fall for those types of men when we really should be dumping them. **"**

Alex has an important point. Many men become scared babies if they can't handle emotions. Running away has become a common M.O. Fear drives many people to react in irrational or unhealthy ways. Scared men do dumb things to protect themselves. Then we powwow with friends to figure out why a guy who came on strong goes cold or disappears—especially if you've both just marveled at how special things are between you. Acknowledging how good it is between you can scare many guys. Going slow lowers the risk. And you can control the pace if you take responsibility and choose to use the brakes when necessary.

Slow Down and Listen to Your Instincts

We've been emphasizing that it's important to go slow when you meet someone you like, no matter how perfect he seems. Often the most perfect guys change the fastest. They come on strong and give you exactly what you crave. But, as you let your guard down after gushing to your friends about how perfect he is, he cools and becomes a different person. It takes time to figure out who he really is and whether qualities that attract you are a facade or genuine. Michael T.F. warns:

> **"** Don't assume that the guy you meet is the real guy. Everyone wants to make a good first impression, and it's not until further down the road that the true personality emerges. Men looking for dates are like Miss America contestants: They'll swear up and down that they're interested in world peace, children, and your mind if they think it will help them win. **"**

A misguided belief is that if we show how much we can do for him, he'll stay. Not so! He'll take and then move to another victim or a woman who values herself and expects proper treatment. And just as we talked about the red flags you should watch out for in men, be careful that you don't send one to a guy you like. Matthew has seen it happen:

> 66 From a man's point of view, when women artificially try to rush things and call every day, it's a red flag. He wonders, 'What is wrong with her?' 99

Don't take a guy seriously until enough time has passed for his actions to show that he treats you well and keeps his word—consistently. In later chapters, we have suggestions for creating a life that makes you appreciate having other things to do besides revolve around him. Then he has no choice but to treat you well if he wants you to make time for him. Teach him what proper behavior is! And give it time. Michael McD. suggests taking it slow:

> 66 Women jump the gun too quickly. They have a few dates and automatically assume the guy is exclusive to them. Or they shut their other options off to some extent. Just be yourself! My motto is 'Slow and steady wins.' Don't rush anything, but don't slow to the point of nearly dead. If you go slow and steady, you'll eventually get to your goals. You'll progress over time and build trust and other things that are important in a relationship. 99

"It's not what men say, it's what they do that women should pay attention to, because men say almost anything. You have to be careful that you're not just listening to what they say and not watching what they're doing."   —Brian

Fear of getting too close can motivate your guy to purposely aggravate you. Sounds crazy? Well, it's called *sabotage*. Men admit that when they're scared they try to push you back by saying or doing something you won't like. Since he may not know how to get less intense, he may annoy you, hoping it will make you pull back but not end it. That's an unacceptable tactic! Like children, guys need boundaries, and it's up to you to set and keep them. Michael M. says:

> **“** Realize that it's a two-way street and that you don't have to accept bad behavior. You can educate the person. Sometimes these guys are used to hooking up with people who let them get away with murder. They're waiting for discipline—someone who respects them enough to say that they're acting badly. That doesn't mean they're bad people or that the relationship is bad, but sometimes you need to drop a line when your guy is acting up. **”**

Don't dive into any man with your eyes closed. After the initial rush of excitement, come up for air to activate your senses. Before getting carried away in a relationship, stop. Breathe. Get into the driver's seat and do something that shows you value yourself! Say "no" instead of going along with everything he wants. If he doesn't want to go to a concert you'd like to attend, go without him instead of skipping it. Make your time just as valuable as his by not always being the one to rearrange your schedule. Be your own person instead of just a reflection of what he'd like you to be. We've come a long way past the mentality of women in past generations. Patrick found a good reminder of how far we've come and encourages you to make the most of it:

> ❝ Browsing through a retro bookstore recently I came upon a title from the 1950s that caused me to first gasp in horror, then laugh out loud: *Dishes Men Like*. Compliments of the good folks at Lea & Perrins Worcestershire Sauce, this cookbook reminded women that their husbands had been hard at work all day (presumably while they were sitting on their asses playing bridge with the ladies auxiliary) and had a God-given right to return home to a plate of runny beef stew. As my lesbian friends are fond of reminding me (ad nauseam), women are no longer bound by obligation to a patriarchal power structure that says marriage is the crowning achievement of their lives. Take full advantage of the strides women have made over the past thirty years. Complete your education, advance your career, or merely enjoy guilt-free sex with any number of suave, would-be suitors. Women have just as much right to sample the goods as men. ❞

Sample, taste, experience, and have fun. Dating more casually provides the best chance of weeding out manipulators and creating a healthy relationship foundation. There are enough ways that men annoy us, without nurturing his inner jerk. Let your positive female strengths keep you out of the arms of a guy who's no good for you. Matthew advises you to go within and use your gut to guide you with men:

> ❝ A strong female strength is intuition—insight and instincts. It's really important for you to draw on that. I'll be hanging out with a woman, and she'll get something right on the head when I didn't

even see it. Women really have to draw into their instincts. If there's something really off with a guy, listen to your instincts. Often you may make excuses, like 'He's calling me now. Everything is great.' But your instincts are waiting for the other shoe to drop. And it does. **"**

You know the signs but choose to ignore them to get some sugar from him. Your instincts will tell you a lot if you listen. The bottom line is if you settle for flowers, compliments, charming excuses, words of love, exciting promises, and all the romantic antics men use to keep us hooked when their behavior isn't good, think about who's accepting the bad behavior in exchange for perks. And if you keep on giving to him unconditionally or put his needs before your own, remember it's your choice, not your obligation.

Before you call him a jerk, look in the mirror and ask "Who's the real jerk?" Men can't be jerks unless we allow them to be. No men are jerks until proven so. If you don't wait for him to prove otherwise, who really is the jerk?

First-Aid Tips

- Write down everything you can think of that men have told you in the past that they never followed though on and things you let them get away with because of something romantic they said or did for you.
- Forgive yourself for being vulnerable when you desire a man.
- Ask a good friend to remind you of why a guy would be lucky to have you.

Reality Check

Going from Fantasy to Realistic Expectations of Men

"I think that women have the fantasy of the white knight, but if the guy can't fulfill that, he becomes the opposite of the white knight."

—Vinnie

We're masters of making excuses for our latest HIM. If he's found your Achilles heel, he feeds you just enough so you'll accept his inexcusable behavior. Do you justify your guy's bad behavior? Women defend inexcusable behavior with statements like "But he doesn't mean to hurt me." DUH! Normally bright, otherwise savvy women become blind to reality when getting fed lines by a guy they like. Take off the rose-colored glasses and see him for who he really is. That gives you the power to change things.

Closing the Book on Prince Charming

Fairy tales in childhood begin the process of creating our image of the Prince Charming we hope to attract as adults. We carry it into adulthood since it seems better than the relationships around us. But Kevin K. suggests you base your expectations on reality and create your own story instead of borrowing one for which you really don't know the ending:

> " The problem is that the story stops before we see who Prince Charming becomes in the fairy tale, once they unite through the magic of a kiss. A couple invested in the fantasy of Prince Charming and his princess have an opportunity to write the rest of the story. But most couples miss that and seek scripts already written—looking to less than desirable role models for patterns to live out a story line rather than grasping the opportunity to create their own happily ever after. "

"HELLOOO, Prince Charming is in a FAIRY tale! (Does that make Prince Charming gay? Hmmm??)"   —Ed

Watching romantic movies starring gorgeous guys who act perfectly and reading romance novels where guys lovingly sweep women off their feet reinforce the image of a modern Prince Charming. These guys are always available, communicate passion with perfect words, create total ecstasy in bed every time and last all night. We get pangs of longing as we absorb this sheer fantasy and want it in real life. These expectations hurt your perspective of a healthy relationship, Patrick warns:

66 It's a biological and psychological impossibility. Wake up and smell the cappuccino! Prince Charming is a fable. Heterosexual men are human and thus have their shortcomings. Adjust your expectations without sacrificing your principles or dignity (unless we're talking about the bedroom, where dignity is but a useless affectation). 99

A writer's imagination creates these guys, not Mother Nature. And yet you still ask "Why can't I find my Prince Charming?" Carl answers:

66 This one's easy: Because it's a FANTASY. If it's OK for you to ask this question, then it should be OK for men to ask 'Why can't women live up to the naughty nurse fantasy?' Besides, have you seen what most guys look like in tights? 99

If fiction turns you on, keep a good stock of romance novels and batteries for your vibrator—the only way to have a storybook romance that doesn't disappoint. Real life can't live up to fiction, and that's okay. If you accept that there's no such thing as Prince Charming, you can then accept that all men come with imperfections, just as you do. It allows you to be realistic in your choice of a partner. A guy who you enjoy being with can make you very happy, even if he likes sports more than you do or doesn't express himself like guys do in movies. Couples who compromise and learn to live with qualities they'd leave out of their fantasies find happiness in appreciating the good stuff they bring to each other. Michael T.F. gets real:

❝ In the real, non-Disney world men leave underwear on the floor, don't care if you reach orgasm, and think going down on you only has to happen on your birthday (which he'll probably forget anyway). The problem with fairy tales and Hollywood movies is they end right at the happiest point, usually the wedding. They don't show you what life is like a month later when Prince Charming is tired of swooping you off his feet and the white horse has crapped all over the castle. ❞

Looking for Prince Charming can be dangerous. It sets you up to fall for guys who know how to perfect their come-on to lure you into bed or a relationship they control to your disadvantage. These manipulators know how to play the role so they can get you into a relationship on their terms. Once they've hooked you, their true colors show but you're already invested. It's hard to leave a manipulator when he's made you convinced that you need him. Eventually most will leave you hurting and wondering why you can't meet a decent man. Keep your expectations reality based for a better chance of meeting one who makes you happy. Michael M. warns:

❝ Prince Charming doesn't exist. There's no perfect person. The expectation that a man should be Prince Charming is unreasonable to live up to. A man can never live up to that. It's the woman's expectations that need to change. Seeing someone in a realistic light is the best way. ❞

Stop making fictitious men and the Prince Charming myth a model for the man of your dreams! That eventually causes nightmares. Having realistic standards for a man who complements your life makes it easier to find someone who makes you happy long-term. Overblown fantasy expectations about romance aren't fair to men, or to you. As we grapple with changing our perception of a relationship and redefining ourselves as empowered women, it's hard to let go of stereotypes as we adopt new ways. So we give men mixed messages. David says men are very confused these days by them:

> **❝** Women want to be equals, but then they want to be a woman. A woman shouldn't want to be rescued. She should want to be loved, respected, and nurtured. If a woman labels what she's looking for as Prince Charming, she has an unrealistic concept of what men can be. **❞**

Our expectations put so much pressure on men. Making them responsible for our happiness and security is a lot to expect from someone! They may not show it directly, but men buckle under that kind of pressure. It may manifest in some of the irrational behavior that drives us crazy. Seeing what you expect of him can make a hot man go cold fast. And since men's communication skills are limited, he might just mumble "Nothing" if you prod him about what's wrong. He may not understand it himself and only knows he can't handle hearing you discuss your future kids or criticize what he considers to be his normal behavior. Try to have more compassion when you dump your needs on him! Matthew advises that making him feel that your security and happiness are in his hands can overwhelm him:

66 Men have kind of a Superman ego issue. They have a lot of stress, just in different ways than women do. We really have to prove ourselves out in the world. You might be coming at it from a Prince Charming point of view. But for him it's more of the Superman problem. What goes through a man's head is 'I already don't make enough money or have enough power at my job. I have to be the fifth monkey down on the monkey ladder at work, and I already have these insecurity masculine issues. And here this woman is telling me I have to do even more. I'm already feeling strung out.' Success, accomplishment, and how other men and women see him is really important to a man. Then a woman comes in and adds to his burden. Women don't see it that way, because they're coming from such a self-centered point of view. I think you really have to understand the problems men have. Of course men have to understand women, too. 99

Spinning Tales: Don't Believe Them!

Excuses are glue that keeps you stuck to a guy who doesn't treat you right. They rationalize away behavior that should be stopped. Think about the logic behind excuses such as these:

- "I know he didn't do what he promised, but he's working hard at his job." He had that job when he made the promise. Next!
- "It hurt when he yelled insults at me, but I know he doesn't mean it. He had a rough childhood, and it affects him." Let him grow up without you!

• "He doesn't understand why his actions bother me." Sure he does. You told him. But he refuses to understand because then he'd have to stop.

"A lot of times men are good with excuses. They think that any amount of horseshit will get them through anything. You have to lay down the law and not accept easy answers." —**Michael M.**

Everyone slips up. But let him sincerely apologize and make it up to you instead of justifying bad behavior with excuses. You want to believe them so he'll stay. The bottom line is we make and accept excuses because being with him on some level is more important than being treated well. That also makes us defend his actions when someone cares enough to question his inappropriate or downright hurtful behavior. Acknowledging that they're right means you should take action. Ouch! That can be a painful idea. So you make excuses for him. Rick explains:

66 It's usually really transparent. People see that you're doing it. They know he's a jerk. It makes you look like a jerk because you're settling for a jerk and covering for him. It also makes you seem weak. Let him speak for himself. Who are you trying to convince: yourself or everybody else? 99

"Read between the lines, honey. Look deeper. There's more to the story than your needing to understand his excuses." —Kevin A.

Learn to distinguish between an occasional action you don't like and a pattern. He'll never be perfect and will do things you don't like. But if he regularly makes excuses for the same type of bad behavior, it becomes a pattern, which shouldn't be accepted. Often excuses are laced with compliments and promises that sound good. Don't buy it! The only acceptable response is a sincere apology followed by good behavior. The longer you let him get away with it, the harder it is to stop the pattern later. Rick explains:

> **❝** A lot of men cruelly know how to push a woman's buttons. They know what you want to hear, so they dangle things in front of you, like 'Well, yes, I did this, but you know that we're going to do this and do that and go here.' They sort of tell you what you want to hear and dangle carrots in front of you to keep you with them. **❞**

"Point out what bothers you and show him a guideline of what he is doing wrong."　　　　　　　　　　　　　　**—Kevin S.**

"Bad meat doesn't regain its freshness just because you stick it back in the fridge."　　　　　　　　　　　　　**—Randall**

It takes time to determine if a guy likes you for you or for making it easy to get his needs met without a lot of effort. He may like doing what he pleases more, even if it hurts you. He'll try to dodge your complaints with an apology cloaked in promises of what he

knows you'd like—that often never materialize. Having expectations he can play into lets him get away with nonsense if you feel
needy for them to be met. Listen to his excuses for bad behavior.
Do you really buy it? Absorb the whole picture of his manipulation.
He knows what he's doing, no matter what he says. If you accept
excuses in exchange for crumbs, write down why you believe them.
If they honestly make sense, stay until he breaks your heart. If you
think with your head for a while, you'll see the excuses for what
they are: manure! Alex says:

> ❝ There will always be pain in relationships. But when there's so
> much that your gut tells you something is wrong, you'd better listen
> because that gut feeling is almost always right. When you feel that
> you're losing respect for yourself in a relationship, that's definitely a
> key moment when you need to start making a move. ❞

"If he's disrespectful, confront him immediately. Or leave. No
excuse!"   —Andy

But I Love Him!

When I give advice on TV talk shows, it astounds me how many
women say "But I love him!" to defend why she won't leave a guy
who hurts her. Over and over, women justify not taking action
against HIM by believing love overrides all else. Rick advises:

66 Really check your definition of what love is or what you think love is, because defending him is not love. It's a desperate need and fear of being alone—and invalid. I think it's anything but love. 99

"If you use love as an excuse, you probably don't have a clue about what love is."   —Kevin S.

What is love? Security? Great sex? Some sweet words or tenderness when he's making yet another excuse for hurting you? Someone to make you feel complete? Love should make you happy, not complete. Curt elaborates:

66 Real love is when you find somebody and can't get them out of your head; when you feel them inside you in a spiritual way; when you worry about them; when you feel that you would do anything for someone—that's love. Love is this warm feeling that you get when you're around this person. When you're having a bad day and you can think of this person, you brighten up. 99

Does being abused, physically or mentally, brighten your day? Is any attention better than none? Love does not make everything else okay! Change your refrain to "I'm using love as an excuse for my inability to take charge of my life and let go of HIM." Or redefine what love really is. Love isn't about how romantic he can be. And it's not about symbols. Real love goes much deeper. Alex explains:

❝ True love isn't buying each other flowers and candy when Valentine's Day rolls around and other ways we misperceive love. Real love is sticking by someone and forgiving them for their faults, having respect for each other in that relationship. That's love. ❞

"You may love him, but that doesn't mean he loves you back. That kind of one-way relationship is a direct road to misery. Take the nearest exit!"   —Randall

Does he show love all the time or just when he placates you after doing something wrong? Pay attention. You deserve great treatment in return for your love. If you can't be honest with others, at least be honest with yourself. Love should never excuse abuse—physically or mentally. True love takes a long time to develop and grow. A big factor that comes with love is trust, which must be earned over a long period of time. Focus on being in like and wait to jump into love when lust or needs aren't clouding your judgment. Kevin S. says:

❝ Supposedly women fall in love faster. They always seem ready for love, and every relationship could potentially be about falling in love. Slow down and find out 'Is this guy worthy of my love?' Why put yourself out in left field? 'I know he's an ass and hasn't called in three weeks, but I love him!' You're so off in left field already. Find someone else. ❞

Get rid of the belief that if you show him enough love he'll become your Prince Charming. If he treats you poorly now, giving him more love won't change that. It can actually reinforce his belief that he can do anything and you'll stay. LOVE SHOULDN'T HURT YOU! It should make you feel wonderful. That's why love in a relationship must be reciprocal. He needs to show you the kind of love you show him, not just say he loves you. Alex adds:

66 Women have a tendency to believe they can love for both of them. If they have enough in a relationship—like it she puts in her part AND the part he's not putting in—then maybe it will survive. I'm sorry to say that does not work. You both have to put in. You can't love someone and then compensate for what he's not doing. Know when to leave. When your integrity is being compromised and you're disrespected, it's very important to leave. 99

Now You See Him—Now You Don't

Have you had an amazing evening with a guy, shared feelings about a variety of interests, felt intense attraction, perhaps shared some intimacy, and then never heard from him again? Or he came on strong for months, saying everything you wanted to hear, being the perfect mate for you, then turned cold and distant or just ended it? Carl explains:

66 It's the thrill of the chase, which must be genetically ingrained in the male species. And the run part? Well, that's the old fear-of-commitment issue. Many men outgrow this stuff as they

grow older, but some don't. Learn how to recognize the confident, stable men who don't need to give you a bunch of lines when they first meet you, only to disappear after Date No. 2. 🎤

"Men want a Re-laid-shionship (not a relationship)."   —Ed

Guys are brave when it comes to killing bugs and watching scary movies. They're chickens about intimacy and getting too hooked. If he's not ready to commit, he may bolt in a way that leaves you reeling and asking what's wrong with men. Michael T.F. has observed that some men go in and out of relationships through a revolving door because they don't want to lose the initial rush and ego boost of connecting with someone new:

66 With most guys it's about making the conquest. They want to know that they can have you. Once they get you, they don't need to prove anything so they move on to the next woman who will prove to them how attractive, smart, funny, and all-around perfect they are. The biggest myth about relationships is that men are afraid of commitment. What men are really afraid of is losing the rush they get when a new woman finds them irresistible. 🎤

So how can you minimize the chance of getting caught in his nonsense? TAKE IT SLOW. Keep the chase going. No one should give everything away in a relationship. Ever! If he comes on strong with a desire to see you constantly, don't succumb, even if it feels delicious to be desired. Hold your ground and keep some distance by continuing to make plans with friends and scheduling solo time. Get friends to tie you down if you begin to revolve around him. He'll be too preoccupied with wondering if you'll stay to get scared of going too fast. Michael McD. explains:

66 People jump the gun, find themselves in something quicker than they wanted, and get scared. Their reaction is to run away, rather than confront it. When you take it at a slower pace, there is more communication, which is 100 percent key for that, and you can talk about issues as you go. At the beginning it's all easy, but then the issues start to come up. Then people start to run. That's usually someone who's not emotionally available. If you're looking for people who are emotionally unavailable, that means you're emotionally unavailable. Something is going on that makes you rush it. 99

When you have other things going on besides him, he doesn't feel as suffocated. Don't fall into the Fantasy Island trap—getting carried away by his enthusiasm. Keep a slower pace. Men who can't control their fast pace begin to feel out of control fast. If that happens, he may leave as you float on the exhilaration of finding the "perfect" boyfriend. Save yourself the pain of the dump and the questions you and your friends will have about "How could he leave that when he was so into me?" Rick warns:

66 Any extreme reaction at the beginning has to really be examined. You have to be able to take a step back and look at

that. As delicious as it might seem, if it's someone you are attracted to, you are sort of welcoming that attention. A wise person would take a step back, look at it, and think 'This is coming from some place else, and I have to figure out what this is before I jump in.' 99

I used to ask why men are such clones of each other when I should have taken responsibility for allowing myself to fall for the double dive at the beginning. It takes two to dive into a relationship. We always blame it on him. But if you're needy for a boyfriend, it's easy to ignore obvious patterns and enjoy the initial ride. When you work on controlling yourself, you won't jump in without thinking. Often when a guy rushes into something, he has a problem. David advises you to keep the brakes on as much as possible, no matter how much you'd love to dive into the goodies he offers:

66 You should start with him being an acquaintance, then a friend, then a best friend, then a boyfriend/lover. After that he's your significant other. It's really important to create a boundary with each one. If you go from acquaintance to lover and he starts exhibiting some crazy behavior, you'll feel hurt. You've exposed yourself and become vulnerable with someone you don't know. If you take time to know him well before becoming intimate and close, the experience during that time helps you communicate better. But most of us go too quickly, and that's when we get hurt. 99

It's Called Lying!

When your guy doesn't tell the truth, he's lying. Making excuses for why he's not telling the truth doesn't make it less of a lie. Don't write off lying by convincing yourself he has a good reason for doing it. Some guys manipulate women with lies, but they only work if you accept them. Yiannis explains:

> 66 A man may lie regardless of what a woman does because, well, some men just lie. That does not mean that you have to make it easy for him. When we let ourselves believe a man's lie, we're not enabling the lie—he's enabling the fantasy world we're living in. You know, the one where he's not cheating on us, not doing drugs, and not an unemployed bum. 99

> "Women are naturally very suspicious, so men have to lie to them in order to have an easier life. If a woman really trusts her man, he would not feel the need to lie."   —Michele

Some men have mastered the art of lying. Women can be such suckers for a well-presented untrue story. You want to believe him! So you suck up words that don't quite feel right to avoid seeing him for the jerk he is. Kyle advises that you pay closer attention to his words and take responsibility for allowing him to lie:

> 66 If you find that your boyfriend has been giving you the same lame excuse continually, you need to evaluate the relationship.

Honesty is one of the most important qualities, and without it a relationship is probably not very healthy. You have to put yourself first and see if the man is giving so much to you that it is acceptable for him to lie. You know that there's nothing that makes lying acceptable, so wake up and get a life! 99

You reinforce lying by accepting lies. Insist on the truth! On the other hand, don't set him up to lie by making it unpleasant for him to tell the truth. We can do that without realizing the consequences. Kevin K. explains:

66 In their possessiveness, women can set a standard of behavior or feeling so high that the guy doesn't have a chance for honesty if he wants to maintain a relationship with the woman. The guy may then lie for survival. 99

Men complain that women try to put unfair restrictions on them. You might be fine about him spending time with his brother but not with friends. If his buddies threaten you, all hell can break loose if he sees one instead of seeing you. He knows it and prefers not to start a scene, especially if it's harmless. Michael A. says:

66 Women set up expectations with a bat in their hands. What they're saying is either give me the right answer or I whack you with the bat. If the guy is in love with the girl—we may be stupid creatures but we're smart rats—he knows what you want to hear.

So we fake by understanding what you expect to hear and give you what you want, whether it's true or not. **"**

> "Women contribute to men's lying by pushing issues that should not be pushed; by being nosy; by flipping out when he comes clean."   **—Andy**

Help him tell the truth. If your guy lies about his activities, consider what your response is when he tells the truth. Lying is never right, but men get scared to tell the truth if they know they'll get an unpleasant reaction from you. If you trust him—and you should if you stay with him—cut him some slack! Don't try to rule what he can and can't do. Alex explains:

" Women ask questions that warrant dishonest answers, such as "Honey, do you think I'm fat?" No caring husband wants to confirm to his sensitive wife that she is indeed getting fat or old or that she's not as pretty as the day they first met, ad infinitum, ad nauseam—especially when their reactions could mean having to spend the night on the couch. So what do they do? Lie. **"**

Make it easier for him to tell the truth, and he'll be more likely to. Work on why you don't trust him and quit asking questions that he hates answering. And be careful about your response to him telling the truth. Michael A. advises:

66 You have to do self-inventory about how passive-aggressive you're being and be brutally honest with yourself. If you let him know that if he doesn't give you the right answer he'll suffer the consequences, accept that you've rigged the system to force him to lie. Then you blame him for being dishonest, but you create the situation. 99

First-Aid Tips

Ignoring hurtful stuff he does doesn't lead to happiness. In later chapters we'll share more details about what you can create within yourself. Meanwhile, here are some of the best tools you can begin developing to protect yourself from men:

• Awareness: Paying conscious attention to how a man treats you is key to keeping jerks at bay. If you're lost in La-La-Land because he's pushing some good buttons, you might not notice all that bad stuff he's getting away with.

• Confidence: The more you feel good about you, the less crap you'll accept from others. Use the tools in this book to build your confidence with men so that your awareness will help you leave if it's not good for you.

• Speak up! You must tell him what bothers you and ask what he can do to make you feel better. The first step is to try to talk about it. You'll know by his response how open he is to making you happy. Listen carefully.

• A life: If you have a life to fall back on, you won't feel so stuck with a guy who does you wrong. We'll tell you how to develop one in Chapter 9. Having a satisfying life on your own helps you leave. Why let anything into your wonderful life that taints it?

• Some gay friends: Cultivate friendships with gay guys if you have the opportunity. They can be the greatest support system and won't accept the bull you give your girlfriends about why you must put up with intolerable behavior.

MEN WILL BE MEN!

How to Work with Men, Not Change Them

"Wait for a guy who's already right for you, as is."
—*Yiannis*

Here's a concept for you to get your reality grasp around: Men are different, not wrong. Do you wish you could turn a guy into your dream man or ask "Why can't men be more like women?" There are no relationship wish fairies! You can only change YOU. Changing your response to how men act can turn around potential jerks. You can give him no choice but to treat you well. Most relationship books tell you how to change men. Not this one! Your best chance of having a satisfying relationship is to change yourself and your response to men. Michael T.F. wants women to understand that they should allow men to think and act differently than women:

    ❝ The most important thing to understand about men is that men are not women. They are always going to be different from you, and there are always going to be things the sexes don't understand about one another. That ongoing mystery is part of what makes heterosexual relationships appealing to both parties. 99

Who gave us the right to determine what should go on in a relationship, without taking into account what men want? You know—women! We collectively make rules that we expect men to follow. Is that fair? NO! Trying to change a man can be futile. If you're waiting for a guy with right-out-of-the-box perfection, buy a Ken doll! Everyone is annoying at least sometimes. Even you!

> "Don't boss him around or let him boss you. A lot of women come in for a haircut and say things like 'I want to cut it short but my husband wants me to keep it long.' A relationship should be a give and take."
>   —Glenn

If You Want to Sculpt, Take a Pottery Class

Do you treat men like clay, ready to mold them into your version of the perfect partner? Chuck that concept if you want a good relationship! Men are people (despite our comparing them to puppies), with feelings (even if they don't show them), preferences (often contrary to ours), and other differences they're entitled to. Keoni warns that trying to change your guy probably won't get satisfying results:

66 You really can't change beer and nuts. If your man understands and likes who he is, then you can't make him be your perfect catch. More to the point, if you manage to change him, he might not like who he becomes, and then you still lose. 99

If you do find someone who lets you mold him, he'll turn moldy fast. An insecure guy does what he's told. But you'll get bored when the novelty wears thin! Guys who do everything to please you can make you yawn after the initial fun of always getting your way ends. Fix yourself instead (more in Chapter 14) and learn to appreciate your guy's nuances, says Michael T.F.:

66 A man is not a house. You can't just change the paint color, add a breakfast nook, or throw some drapes on the windows. Trying to turn someone into the perfect guy is like buying a fixer-upper and then complaining that the floors sag a little and the roof leaks during storms. Sometimes the faults are part of the appeal. 99

"Like Play-Doh, we're not going to stay for long in the shape you put us in." —Michael A.

Your man is an equal partner and entitled to equal rights, no matter what your girlfriends say. If he annoys you—leave. Or get used to him. Besides, trying to change his essence rarely works, so save your energy. No matter how much he loves you, he'll rarely change everything you want! If yours is a really tasty cheesecake, push the strawberries aside if you don't like them. Enjoy the cake itself, as a tasty dessert for your life. Let him keep his berries! Dan explains:

66 Women don't realize that once you're in your mid-twenties, you probably won't change that much. Some get into relationships thinking it's great and wonderful, and that the baggage somebody has will disappear, but in most cases it doesn't. You've got to tell yourself to accept it as a factor or not accept it and find somebody else. You're doomed to disappointment if you expect a man will have a massive change of character. 99

Men don't come with warranties. One can't be exchanged for another of the same model if you determine he's defective. You must accept him as is. Warts and all. A man will always do at least some things differently than you want him to, and it's his right to be who he is—like it or not. Beliefs that he'll change once he falls for you and you get your hands on him in a relationship are unrealistic. Carl cautions:

66 You're not buying a dress here. While a really expert seamstress can make alterations to a dress to make it fit, don't expect the same miracles with a live human being. For something as important as a relationship, isn't it worth trying to find something that fits right off the rack? Don't expect the perfect fit, of course, and minor tweaks and training can be applied as the relationship grows. But Mr. Slob isn't likely to become Mr. Clean after you get married. 99

Distinguish between annoying and unacceptable behavior. Leaving dishes in the sink or not sharing feelings is annoying. Lying or being disrespectful is unacceptable. Be vigilant of disrespectful behavior but more tolerant of what annoys you, unless you prove that you're perfect. And accept that just because you don't like his way, it doesn't make him wrong. Kevin K. advises you to lighten up on making a man your project:

66 Many women say they are looking for a soul mate. But, when they get a real man, their attitudes and behavior betray a deeper desire, which is for an anatomically correct mannequin, with a robotic voice box that tells them what they want to hear, when they want to hear it. You may enjoy the remake job, but he will only experience hell. The perfect catch will be quite imperfect. At least some of the joy in the relationship is in the growth that comes through tackling the imperfections. If the faults seem unbearable, the catch was the wrong one. 99

"Men never advance beyond the age of nine. We are all nine-year-old boys inside. We like movies where things blow up, we think people falling down and getting hurt is funny, and we touch ourselves as often as possible."   —Michael T.F.

Learn from men! They're not all wrong, no matter what your friends decide. People say that I think a lot like a guy these days because I love my space and independence. I think that's good, since I still enjoy being feminine too! When you develop good self-esteem and create a happier life, your tolerance for a man's harmless ways increases.

Stop Trying to Control Him!

As women fight for equality, we try to control relationships. We can put ourselves on autopilot to prod our latest HIM to be the man we want. It never works. Badgering him into doing things your way can scare a guy away. Harping never turns a man into a perfect pretzel. Some bend a little but eventually snap back and leave. No one likes to feel unacceptable as they are. Since a man's ego can be fragile, men feel whipped when you find fault with everything, explains Michele:

66 Nowadays women are very strong—not only because of their human nature but also speaking professionally. They have such a massive influence in modern society that it scares men. Yes, I think men are scared, and this provokes distance. Women need to understand that, keep the power for themselves, and let men believe they are the best and they need them. Men need to feel strong, macho, even if they are not anymore. 99

Many guys do want to please you. BUT—they also must be true to themselves. We have many levels of things we want from them—validation, security/money, constant attention, marriage, and kids. Men want less. Men are simpler than women are. Our agendas run rings around theirs. For most men give him sex regularly, feed him, maybe do his laundry and clean sometimes, let him watch sports, and don't nag him, and he's on Fantasy Island. Michael McD. warns that you love him with conditions if you can't accept him for who he is:

66 Trying to change someone is a control issue. You have to accept that we can't control people. And we can't change people. The only person we have control over is ourself. If there is something you are unhappy with personally, then work on that. You can't mold other people to what you are looking for. Find people who fit what you're looking for and are really that way by their nature. 99

Our more complex needs can overwhelm him. Just because he doesn't do something your way doesn't mean he's wrong or doesn't care about you. His priorities may just be different. You draw inspiration from friends, books, and classes. It's harder for men to know what to do when you complain. They interpret many of our actions as trying to control them. Keoni explains that men like to do, and one of the best things you can do is specifically tell him what you need done:

66 If you want to just share an experience or problem, talk to a girlfriend. Men love to think, to build, to fix. If you want him to be a part of your life and activities, let him 'be' who he is and give the man something to do. Just keep the 'honey do' list in the do-able range. 99

"Women want to show that they're useful and can contribute. For instance, a woman might go over to her guy's place and tidy up a little. A lot of guys get territorial and think that the tidying up is messing with their system."   —Fritz

Many men are proud of how they show a woman love, until she cuts him down because it's not what she wanted. Many give up. They need loving guidance, not nagging and criticism. For your own sake, please accept that men don't have to change. Men aren't in touch with the details of dating like we are and often ignore feelings and hints. While theirs isn't the best way, it's not our place to fix them. David explains:

66 Men and women will never be complete equals because they're different. Most men cannot articulate their emotions to the degree that women do, nor do they want to most of the time. That's just the nature of primitive man. 99

Men Don't Share Feelings

Guys get frustrated at their inability to let go and share feelings. They know it might be healthier to do so, but they find women too emotional to learn from. One of the most troublesome differences between men and women is our expression of and response to feelings. As a guy learns to trust you, he'll open up more. Matthew believes patience goes a long way to getting him to that point:

" Men have stronger issues about weakness, and showing weakness, as part of the male culture. If they don't keep their cool, they lose points with their peers. So men feel they need to keep their cool so they don't run with their feelings in the obvious way women do. We see feelings as a weakness, where women see them as a strength, so that's a basic cultural difference between the sexes. Men feel, 'When I'm in the mood to show my feelings I will, but when I'm not in the mood I won't.' That gets into a vicious cycle where you sense the man pulling back when it's just the mood that he's in. Then you try to chase him further, which makes him retreat further. It's what they call the 'male cave.' I'll sometimes go for three or four days without picking up the phone when I'm in my cave. If a woman or a buddy is in his face 24/7, it turns a guy off. If men could verbalize things better, women would handle it better. But we aren't in touch with our feelings and don't always even know what we're feeling. So when we go into our caves, it can mean that we're trying to sort out whatever is going on, on a subconscious level. It can be as simple as that. You need to understand that's a weakness in men. "

"Men are just as emotional as women are, but society tells them not to show it. Women have been taught it's okay to be emotional and accept being pampered." —Michael McD.

Don't make it harder by expecting too much. Let him be emotional in his own way. Most guys will never share with you the way you share with your girlfriends and gay friends. And that's okay. If he shares a little, we often want more, without appreciating that he's trying. Men get shot down for not opening up enough. Then they clam up, and frustration continues. If he shares even a teensy bit, let him know you appreciate him trying. He may try harder next time. Keoni advises that you ask yourself why it's so important to get your guy to open up more:

66 If it is so you can feel closer and more connected, then don't. If you need to feel emotionally connected and flowing, then talk to your favorite girlfriend, female, or gay guy. If he is emotionally struggling with something you can share with him, help him through without his divulging every torrid detail. Those details will only keep him more separate from you later. 99

Try to restrain yourself—don't complain that it's not enough. If you allow him to open up as he gets comfortable, it will happen slowly—better than not at all. Meanwhile, get used to him and stop making a big deal! Vinnie advises:

66 Being emotional is a foreign language to straight men. Women push too hard and want them to share their emotions right away. Women establish emotional intimacy rather quickly. Everything in the culture tells men to have a thick skin and not be emotional. So you have to go slow. You should encourage men to be more emotional. Straight men are shut down. That's probably why gay guys and straight women are such great friends. A lot of gay guys wear their hearts on their sleeves. It's easy for me to speak about myself and what I'm feeling. I have no shame about that. Straight men do. 99

"Men need their caves. That's why they have a garage or tool shed."
—Matthew

The differences between men and women and how emotional or communicative they are, or are not, has been debated ad nauseam. But according to Alex, we should focus more on what we have in common:

66 There's a tendency to believe that men are more practical than women are and that women tend to make decisions based more on emotions. They're not so different from each other; they're all human beings. Instead of putting up a barrier of the sexes between males and females, you can find a lot of common ground if you keep your eyes open. 99

We really are all human beings. If you can't live with him as he is, move out! In Chapter 8 we'll give you tips on gently nudging him to improve. But if you have big problems with his ways, he's not for you. Trying to mold him into the image of what you want won't do any good. Travis agrees:

66 I have had my fair share of charity cases where the problem was more like I don't see what they all see . . . that this guy is not going to change and trying to force him to is not going to work! The perfect example I have is this couple that I knew. One was totally into sports and he LOVED football. Every Sunday he would camp out in front of his TV to watch the games, and his boyfriend

would always try to talk him into going to see a play or something really artsy. Neither one of them would give in, and they ended up breaking up with each other because neither could force the other one to do what he liked. Well, that, and the fact that they had a huge fight about one of them wanting to watch the Emmys while a Chargers game was still on. Find a guy whose faults you fall in love with, whether it is his obsession with a daytime soap or college football. You don't have to like it, just respect it and enjoy it because it's part of what makes him who he is. **"**

Most Straight Men Hate to Shop, and It's OK

Do you love shopping? Most straight men don't. Yet many of us insist on schlepping the poor guys along on shopping trips. Why do we drag them? Do we need them to validate our purchases? Or is it that we can't live without them for a few hours? Leaving him home is often a gift of love to him, and you. Alex explains:

" We've all seen them in women's shoe stores, lingerie boutiques, and perfume emporiums: those bored men who sit patiently inside these stores, holding purses while their wives shop. Women should understand that no matter how involved and caring their men may be, most do not like to spend hours at a time picking china patterns or choosing between trendy handbags. It would be just as unfair if a man expected his wife to spend her day tagging along with him while he shops for power tools at the local hardware store. 〞

"It seems that if your man has no interest in shopping, it's a great time to spend with your girlfriends, or even better with one of your gay male friends, who understands that shopping is the elixir of life." —Kevin K."

If you need something for both of you, plan to only shop for that—quickly. Leave your personal shopping for another time. You don't need to get his opinion on things you try on. If he's there begrudgingly, he'll just give you lip service to get out fast. And you'll know it. What's the point! Enjoy shopping and surprise him by wearing something nice that you bought. If you must ease him into shopping, give it to him in small doses. Patrick says:

❝ Most straight men abhor shopping. Test the waters by buying him an article of clothing: a sporty dress shirt, a pair of dress slacks or loafers. Slowly gauge his comfort level with your choices. This might eventually spark an interest in him doing his own shopping—but don't count on it. 〞

Girlfriend Alert

Sometimes our girlfriends are the worst ones to get advice from about guys. Even when they mean well, many encourage you to manipulate men and do everything your way. When women get together to discuss men, Ed says, they make joint decisions based on what they'd like, and they set it down as law:

66 Girlfriends make it seem like a 'War Plan' and start to talk 'RULES' and tactics and other things that take away from the enjoyment of dating and make it a LOT of work! I know. I watched *Sex and the City* AND *Girlfriends*. 99

"Whining to other women is like the blind leading the blind."
—Vinnie

Our girlfriends pressure us to maintain the standards in dating that suit our own needs. The trouble is, many judgment calls are based on anger toward men because of their own bad experiences. If something your guy does reminds your friend of a guy who did her wrong, she'll plot to put yours in his place to get even. Watch the girlfriend advice, warns Michael McD.!

66 While it comes with good intentions, people project their own past experiences when they give advice. So, they're not always giving you the right advice because it's based on themselves. People are often on power trips. When they don't see the whole side of a situa-

tion, they may look out for what they see as your best interest, but it may not be the best thing for you to do. It's difficult to stay objective as a friend. Of course you're interested in your friend's well-being, but it may not always be the right advice. Learning how to trust and follow your own instincts is the best way. Asking too many people for advice can cloud your own judgment—you're spreading yourself around too much and looking for answers in other people when you need to search in yourself for the right answers. 99

Do you keep asking friends for advice until you hear the answer you want? Your sensible friends might tell you to chill, but you might not want to. So you talk to enough girlfriends to find one who encourages you to do what you want to, even if your gut knows it's wrong. In general, women tend to analyze too much. And our girlfriends join in. Guys don't do that. Rick explains:

66 I find that a lot of women really overanalyze every move a man makes. You don't have guys sitting around in a room wondering if they are mad at each other like women do. Men are more straightforward. It goes back to the organs being external and internal. Women seem more complicated and internal, whereas men let it hang out there. 99

We need to trust our instincts more. Girlfriends can only go by what you say and are not always objective. Perhaps some underlying envy clouds the advice. It's difficult to listen to yourself. It's hard to do that if you're used to asking every friend what she thinks. But you must! Michael T.F. says:

66 Your girlfriends, in general, either want to sleep with your boyfriend or can't imagine why you would want to sleep with him. If they want to sleep with him, they're going to try to get you to dump him. If they can't imagine why you would want to sleep with him, they're going to try to get you to dump him. You're better off trusting your dog to (help you choose a guy). If your dog doesn't like a guy, dump him. Dogs are never wrong. 99

When you do get advice from friends, know who it's coming from. Figure out which friends you can trust and who has a lot of bitterness toward men. Choose your advisors wisely! If you surround yourself with friends who constantly say that you need a man, consider developing more powerful female friendships.

"If they're jealous, friends may give bad advice. If you have too many friends, they may confuse you. Listen to yourself."   —Andy

Translating Man Speak

"Men don't communicate. Men tell."   —Michael T.F.

It should be a no-brainer that men communicate differently than we do. Yet we persist in acting like men don't know how to communicate at all. It's time to accept that men don't have to communicate according to our rules! As you read earlier, pushing him to open up makes him shut down. You can't nag him into submission, though many of us try. Men say we make them clam up with our attitudes of superiority about communication. They're not comfortable sharing but would try harder if we let them. Help the poor puppies by learning to compromise, explains David, and by not expecting too much:

66 A woman needs to create the environment for her man to feel comfortable enough to expose who he really is. Ask him how he feels. And really listen. Don't tell him how to feel or that what he's feeling is wrong or that his communication is not right. Tell him you don't quite understand what he's trying to say and ask if he can explain it a little bit better so you can understand exactly how he feels. Let him know it's okay to tell you. You have to be his friend too. Talk to him the way you'd want to be talked to if you were in that position. Ask yourself 'How would I want to be approached if someone wanted to ask me some intimate questions? What would I want him to say?' Remember not to say or do anything that will hurt the line of communication. 99

Get to really know your guy. Talk with him, not at him. Put yourself in his shoes—as a person who doesn't understand how to answer some chick yakking at him at full speed. ZOOM—your mouth races on as he stammers like an idiot, trying to ignore some and absorb enough so it will eventually stop. Remember—simple. That's men. Say one thing without tons of details and he'll listen.

Dump too much on him and he leaves mentally. Michael McD. clarifies:

> 66 Men don't have a need to make a big deal or talk about things as much as women. Women tend to dwell on things more than men. Men try to avoid things more. A woman tends to obsess on the negative and a man will brush it off more. Women tend to harp on a subject longer than a man. Men can find that irritating. Say what you have to say. Keep it to that. Try to make him comfortable about talking to you and saying what he needs to say. 99

Here's a shocker—men do hear us the first time. But, if they don't give us instant gratification—the response we want—we repeat and repeat and repeat. We call it repeating until he gets it. Men call it nagging. Most of us believe that if we say it enough, it will sink in. The opposite is true. The more you go on, the more he regresses to childhood, reminded of rules and directions repeated over and over by Mommy. Resentment clogs his ears. He usually hears you the first time but won't acknowledge it if he disagrees or doesn't know what to say. Or he may not say what you hoped for. Often our quest for the response we want prevents us from truly listening to him. But you must, advises Michael McD.:

> 66 Listen to him. A lot of women do so much talking—they should learn to listen. A lot of men try to communicate but the women aren't listening. They sometimes hear it but don't take men seriously or are so busy going on and on that they're not listening to what the other person has to say. Listen to what the guy says

and take him seriously. Don't draw conclusions on your own. If you're unclear about anything, it's better to question it and get full clarity. Make conclusions based on that clarity. 🙶🙶

Yak—yak—yak! We're so busy with our own yammering that we often write off what he says, especially if he's not communicating according to our agendas. If a guy knows that you're actively listening with respect for his feelings, he may try harder. Less said often gets more across. Men have limits on what they can absorb at one time and how much they can say. If he's trying to communicate, let him know with touch and the way you look at him that you appreciate it. Tons of words may go through his head with no absorption. Mike explains:

🙶🙶 Men really do have a hard time expressing ourselves to the ones we love, whether we're gay or straight. Your man might not tell you as much as you would like that he loves you, but he does. Also, we don't think as deeply or as often as you do on something! 🙶🙶

"Men have a harder time opening up because women never shut up. Talking and listening are important. The culture that we live in doesn't foster listening. I have to be quiet in my relationship with my partner because I tend to dominate and I have to let him talk."

—Brian

Saying nothing is hard for us. Practice! You can say a lot with actions, touch, and looks. We need to get more comfortable with silence, which can seem like a hole that needs to be filled. But silence really can be golden. It gives you a chance to look him in the eyes, touch tenderly, kiss, and just be with him. Silence isn't an enemy to kill with words. When you get comfortable with yourself, and let go of your need to control HIM, silence feels peaceful. Communication is whatever gets a message across. Gestures do that too. Lovingly share your own feelings. Ed says:

> **“** OH MY GOD! Communication is an entire course at NYU, isn't it? It's all about what's being said combined with what's NOT being said. A lot is said by saying nothing! Open up to him (without the sole purpose being him opening up to you). If you put love out there in an open and honest form, it will come back to you. **”**

Do you accept it if he disagrees with you? Or do you keep trying to change his mind because you need him to understand why you're right? Women defend their barrage of words with "I need him to understand." Do you think if you repeat yourself enough, he'll acknowledge that you know better? Please recognize that if repeating yourself a lot still doesn't get the desired response, he doesn't want to give it. Period! Men aren't as dumb as you think. They've learned to shut their mouths when put on the spot.

"Men have a sort of Windows operating system. The interface looks like it's listening, but behind the motor there's something completely different going on." —Michael A.

Do you judge him for his inability to communicate "properly"? Using a style you don't like doesn't make him wrong. If you need more details, NICELY ask him to explain. If necessary, bite your tongue so he can speak without being interrupted. And—this is a big one—if he makes even a small attempt, encourage him. We can have unfair expectations. He shares a little, but we want a lot. Rather than appreciate his attempts, we knock him for what he hasn't done yet. We shoot down his efforts and kiss any chance of future communication good-bye! Instead, let him know that while you'd like more, you appreciate that he's trying. Reinforce him and he may give a little more next time. Let him open up slowly. Kevin K. says that patience and encouragement can work:

66 Good communication happens incrementally as two people come to know and trust each other. One way is through a discussion of what really interests him. Also, request time for what really interests you. So much of communication is founded in a respect of one person for the other. 99

The guys say straight men regularly complain about how women make a big deal out of things that don't seem important. Women complain that guys don't get the obvious. Obvious to your girlfriends, maybe, but not to him. Be clear about what you want.

What's important to you may not be to him. But guys will respect your feelings if you explain without emotions and don't demand that he agree. When you ask for help, he needs specific chores. Tell him without making it sound like an order. Speak to him like an adult. While men can act like little tykes, they are grownups. Don't bring your guy back to the childhood lectures he got, urges Michael McD.:

66 Sometimes when you try to communicate in a relationship it turns into this parent/child communication. There isn't always the respect of another adult. Guys don't like that. They don't like to be told what to do or talked down to. Women sometimes have a tendency to do that. That's a power trip or control issue thing. And, it loses sight that the guy you're with is an adult. He's your equal and not someone you talk down to. You don't want him to talk down to you! It's easy to lose sight of that, but it's important because the way a message comes across is a huge indication of what you'll get in the long run. 99

Be kinder in your communication, and accept his right to disagree. Men sometimes clam up if they believe you won't like what they think. They're more straightforward, less tactful, and may blurt out something that will annoy or upset you. Don't attack him for it. Learn that there are things you may not want to ask. Michele's insight:

66 I believe men are much more direct and sometimes just too much, but this is in their nature, their instinct. I would first

make sure that a woman could deal with too much information from her partner. **"**

> "Don't ask men any questions you can't handle the answer to."
> —Ed

Men will probably never express feelings like our girlfriends do. But be careful what you wish for. Some women who've experienced an emotional guy complain about feeling nauseated by it. When a guy cries, it's hard to know what to do. Small doses of emotional sharing are delightful in a straight guy. It shows he trusts you. But when men get soft and cloying, it can be a giant turnoff. You may find yourself wondering if he needs therapy to get over it or if he's gay.

Stop Nagging Him Already!!

> "If you're trying to get rid of somebody, that's the perfect recipe. Nag away."
> —Rick

We have three words for you about nagging. DON'T DO IT! Some women are class-A nagging machines who whine complaints at any man who doesn't run from them. Pay attention to what you sound like when you get on a guy's case. It's not a pretty sound. Listen to yourself talk when you're upset with him. Would you like that tone directed at you? Probably not! Make an effort to break the habit. It can take a while but can be done. Vinnie cautions:

66 There's nothing more unattractive than whining or nagging. If nagging is trying to get a man to do something that he didn't initially want to do, it won't work. No one wants to do what they don't want to do, and no one wants to hear about it like that 99

Michael M. agrees:

66 Nobody wants to hear their wife turn into their mother. It brings back horrible childhood memories, like 'Clean up your room. Do your homework.' Neither gender should be a nag. It doesn't sound like you're on your partner's side. You sound like an antagonist. 99

Start listening to yourself if you get frustrated at times when he's not doing what you want him to do and you try to explain how you feel. I doubt that you really want to sound like you do when you're droning on, trying to convince him to do or see it your way. Do whatever you can to break that habit! Besides relaxing with him, it will help you relax with yourself. Matthew warns that you have to see things from a guy's perspective too:

66 Men don't like to be put on the spot. Men like to let things kind of organically happen. It's important to understand how men approach things. It's almost like a different culture. As a travel writer, when I travel to different countries, I try to look at things through their eyes, so there are no misunderstandings. You should do that too! 99

First-Aid Tips

- Take a pottery class if you want to sculpt.
- Write down all the qualities that you don't care for. Star those you absolutely can't tolerate in a man. Ask yourself what you can do to accept the rest in someone who makes you happy in most ways.
- Go to a place that you usually go to meet men with the intention of NOT meeting anyone that night. Talk to as many people as possible, just to have fun. One night without being in your hunting mode won't kill you.

READER/CUSTOMER CARE SURVEY

We care about your opinions! Please take a moment to fill out our online Reader Survey at **http://survey.hcibooks.com**.

As a **"THANK YOU"** you will receive a **VALUABLE INSTANT COUPON** towards future book purchases as well as a **SPECIAL GIFT** available only online! Or, you may mail this card back to us and we will send you a copy of our exciting catalog with your valuable coupon inside.

(PLEASE PRINT IN ALL CAPS)

First Name		MI.		Last Name	

Address					

State	Zip	Email		City	

1. Gender
☐ Female   ☐ Male

2. Age
☐ 8 or younger
☐ 9-12   ☐ 13-16
☐ 17-20   ☐ 21-30
☐ 31+

3. Did you receive this book as a gift?
☐ Yes   ☐ No

4. Annual Household Income
☐ under $25,000
☐ $25,000 - $34,999
☐ $35,000 - $49,999
☐ $50,000 - $74,999
☐ over $75,000

5. What are the ages of the children living in your house?
☐ 0 - 14   ☐ 15+

6. Marital Status
☐ Single
☐ Married
☐ Divorced
☐ Widowed

7. How did you find out about the book?
(please choose one)
☐ Recommendation
☐ Store Display
☐ Online
☐ Catalog/Mailing
☐ Interview/Review

8. Where do you usually buy books?
(please choose one)
☐ Bookstore
☐ Online
☐ Book Club/Mail Order
☐ Price Club (Sam's Club, Costco's, etc.)
☐ Retail Store (Target, Wal-Mart, etc.)

9. What subject do you enjoy reading about the most?
(please choose one)
☐ Parenting/Family
☐ Relationships
☐ Recovery/Addictions
☐ Health/Nutrition
☐ Christianity
☐ Spirituality/Inspiration
☐ Business Self-help
☐ Women's Issues
☐ Sports

10. What attracts you most to a book?
(please choose one)
☐ Title
☐ Cover Design
☐ Author
☐ Content

TAPE IN MIDDLE; DO NOT STAPLE

FOLD HERE

Comments

6

BEWARE HIS SOUTHERN HEAD MENTALITY

Skills to Avoid Sexual Mishaps

*"A lack of respect for the testosterone
imperative either ends the relationship
or converts it into a morgue for the barely alive."*
—Kevin K.

Men think with two heads; women with one. Men are often distracted to the southern region when they experience stimulation they can't control. Once they get aroused, they have to deal with the erection. While some of us also make poor decisions based on sexual desires, men get more carried away. But you can improve your knowledge of geography and learn to respond to men in ways that keep them in check. Accept from the get-go that men often can't help being horny. They have a right to want sex and also to do what they can to get it. It's YOUR choice whether or not you give in. We'll show you how to own your sexual power instead of being a victim to HIS. It begins by understanding AND accepting men as they are.

Erection Deflection

Most men don't mean any harm when they desire sex. To them, their desires are a need to relieve horniness. They don't realize that the object of their lust is analyzing (often with the help of her friends) his touch, assuming he has more feelings than he does, taking every word seriously, and making much more out of a sexual scenario than it is. We hold sex in more romantic terms than men do. We interpret every move he makes as something special. Then if he falls asleep after sex, we're insulted. Men and women tend to respond differently to horniness, and that's okay. Fritz explains:

> ❝ I think to some degree guys are just hardwired. If you think about any other species on the planet, the female of that species is always looking for the best provider and protector, and guys are looking for the top female but are also looking to get their seed around as much as possible. Whether they act on it or not, they'll always have a wandering eye. ❞

Many women aren't nearly as in touch with their sexual needs as men are. We've been taught that it's not nice to consider jumping a guy's bones for the sheer purpose of "getting some," the way guys do. So we're judgmental when they do it to us. Men try to get as much as they can, but they won't succeed if you don't let them. That's part of your power. But you also have the power to own your sexuality. Michael M. says:

66 Women are more emotional than guys. This comes from society's programming of what a man's and a woman's roles are. I don't think men are less emotional than women or that women are less sexual than men. It comes down to what our upbringing programmed. **99**

"Men are sexual. If you're dating a man, you need to remember this. No defense needed—use it. Be strong; take the upper hand and flirt."   —Andy

Many of us do take the upper hand and flirt, but in the same way guys don't want to admit having emotional responses, it's hard for us to acknowledge that sometimes we'd kill to get laid. If you want it and can handle him bolting after, go for it! Most of us prefer sex with someone we're involved with in some sort of relationship. It's best not to make quick decisions. When you're under the influence of him pushing all the right buttons, you can weaken. Come up for air and take time to think. There's no reason to feel guilty if you don't give in to his pressure and the manipulative questions he might throw you like "I thought you really liked me. Why won't you do this?" Or "Don't you trust me?" Shout "NO!" When it comes to getting sex, says Bob, men can be more manipulative than ever:

66 Men tend to live in locker rooms—literally and in their own brains. They believe, mistakenly, that conquest is their natural right, and scoring presumes they know what they're doing—even though they privately realize that women control what, who, when, where, and how about sex in the first place. **99**

Control a man's desire by controlling yourself. Learn to recognize manipulation! Accept that if a guy can get it up, he's going to look for someone to stick it in. If you don't open your legs, he can stick it in his hand. Fritz says:

66 When you get down to it, men are all out for the same thing. It depends on whether they're dogs or not. Guys are going to try to figure out what they need to say to make you feel the way they want you to feel. They're going to try to push all the buttons to get what they want from you. It's all a game to them in some ways. Most want another notch on the bedpost. **99**

In Chapter 3 we warned about the manipulation tools guys use in general—sweet words, flowers, promises, expression of feelings, and so on. These become more pronounced when he's horny. Watch out. Your warning system should be at high alert when a guy tries to wear you down to have sex with him. Pay attention. You can learn to distinguish between a guy who just wants to get laid (who will change his tune and bolt once he's sated) and a horny one who really likes you. The latter will respect that you want to wait to become intimate. The jerk will try to make you feel guilty for not jumping in fast by questioning your feelings for him and being relentless in his quest. The guy who really likes you will wait it out while the jerk will leave sooner. Kevin K. explains:

    66 The testosterone imperative drives a man in ways that I think few if any women can appreciate. It is one that men need to be respected for instead of shamed and ridiculed about. The survival of relationships depends on a respect for it. It speaks significantly about where the guy is in his own maturing process. This doesn't mean I think you should necessarily give up on him; this just gives you significant data. Too often women get involved in trying to fix this in men rather than listening to it. Perhaps if there is to be a happy ending, this is a time for you to spend less time trying to fix the guy's commitment or intimacy issues and more time becoming the seductress. You may find you really enjoy the dating ritual that can ensue. But you really need to know when to give up and look for a different rooster in a different barnyard. **99**

It's a natural instinct for guys to look at attractive women, and there's nothing wrong with that. There's no need to get jealous. It wouldn't hurt you to check out some hot guys too! Just because a guy is with you doesn't mean his sexuality is dead out of your bedroom. LIGHTEN UP about stuff like this. It's okay to look without touching. When your self-esteem is strong, you'll worry less (more in Chapter 14). Jealousy boosts his ego. Why do that? Let him have his bits of fun and show why he's got the best. Threats won't prevent him from cheating if he's inclined to. Giving him some breathing room helps him feel he still has freedom to be a man. He'll be a happier camper if you don't tighten a leash. Happier campers are less likely to cheat. Randy says:

66 Chances are that the man in your life likes to admire pretty waitresses, watch pornography, and spend some time alone with himself, if you know what I mean. Women are wired differently, and they often feel threatened or offended by a man who doesn't devote every last ounce of his interest in females to them. Yes, sometimes men do have affairs with the women they see passing by. Yes, too much porn watching or masturbation can be a sign of trouble. But if you have no other reason to question your man's faithfulness or passion for you, let him admire the passing scenery and meet his sexual needs on his own once in a while. 99

Sex Is NOT a Tool!

Have you ever used sex as leverage to get your way? MANY men complain that their ladies hold sex over their heads to get them to do something. That's crap! Sex is a beautiful act between you and your partner. It's not a bone for a good puppy.

If you're in a monogamous relationship, sex should be an integral part of the intimacy that keeps it strong. If you use it as a bargaining chip, you demean the act. You also tell your guy that you don't value him as a sex partner, since you can do without if he's not a good boy. That's hurtful. If you don't crave your guy, why are you with him? Rick warns:

66 If you're not giving it to him and are holding it over his head and using it as a weapon, it kicks the door wide open for him to go

find it elsewhere. He's just taking care of a need that you wouldn't take care of for him. That gives a man the perfect license to find it elsewhere. If you want to keep a guy by using sex, you had better be better than anybody—a gymnast, the Cirque du Soleil of sex, if that's what you're going to use to keep him dangling. 🎵🎵

"Even though men are dogs, they shouldn't be treated as such. You reward dogs with a treat when they're good. Women do the same thing with sex. It says a lot about their value as a person."   —Brian

Don't use sex to manipulate! The guys emphasized that a good relationship isn't about game playing. A healthy one should never be based on manipulation. Don't you hate when he does that to you? Nobody likes being manipulated. But with men, when you regularly withhold intimacy to get your way, it brings a guy back to childhood, when Mom took away playtime or dessert if he didn't listen.

Well, if you want men to act less like little boys than they do, don't treat them that way! Reward YOURSELF with sex. Appreciate it for the amazing pleasure it is—for you too. Don't demean sex by using it as a weapon. Develop a satisfying sex life and find other ways to compromise about what bothers you. Using sex for manipulation purposes is destructive to a good relationship, warns Matthew:

66 Using sex to manipulate is the height of dishonesty. What is your relationship built on? BS! He'll resent you for it and start screwing around with other women. Women come at it from a victim point of view. 'I have to manipulate him in this passive-aggressive way because that's the only way I'll get what I want out of this.' No! No! No! Guys can smell that a mile away. 99

Love Me Tender—BUT Then Don't Leave Me

Have you ever marveled at a guy who gave you all the tenderness, compliments, promises, and affection you could have wished for in bed? Gentle caresses, loving words, light kisses, emotional responses? But after he seemed so loving in bed, you spend months analyzing with your friends about how he could be so into you and then disappear.

> "Men feel they have to hit all these buttons or you won't put out."
> —Matthew

Men don't think about the details of what goes on during sex like we often do. When they're on their way to an orgasm, most don't think at all. They just do what gets them there best. And if romance gets them there, whatever! A big red flag that we hate to recognize as one is when a man says "I love you" very quickly. It's delicious to hear, but it takes time to fall in love. In most cases, that red flag is telling you that he's either (1) a player—using "I love you" to get more of what he wants; (2) emotionally unstable and says those words whenever a woman makes him feel good; or (3) has strong feelings and blurts out "I love you" without thinking, and it will probably scare him. Don't say "I love you" back if you have even a shred of doubt that it's appropriate. It's up to you not to go over the moon with an interpretation of his moves or what he says. Alex advises that the key to doing this is to be a little skeptical:

66 You should never trust men! If he tells you at first that he loves you and that you're this or that on the first night, you shouldn't feel comfortable with that person. Men can be tender and truthful in expressing tenderness, but don't read into it when the relationship is so young. In the beginning, you don't know if it will be a relationship or where it's going. You can't take anything they say to heart or hold them to it. You have to wait to see if he sticks it out. 99

Men give us delicious goodies since they know how we eat it up, and then eat him, in the golden glow of tenderness and caring. But the boys more often mean it in the moment, while we project to the future. He may really have tender, loving feelings when his member is hard and may really like you—then. But when he gets out of bed, he switches gears and gets cool. It's up to you not to take HIM seriously. You CAN'T hold a man accountable for what he says in the heat of an orgasm. He may say "I love you," but that might mean he loves you at that moment. Afterward, reality sets in. Don't read more into it than the good night of sex it was. Jason puts it this way:

" Men have one face and then they rip it off and become someone else. Some men do it on purpose to get women to sleep with them or feel the challenge of it. Women should be honest and make their own decisions. You need to go slow. Sex has nothing to do with real life. "

"Tenderness, alas, implies nothing except that the man is a better lover than most. And the reverse should be noted as well: Caring men can be lousy in the sack." —Randall

The better you know a guy, the more you can discern fact from fiction. Your guy may be what he thinks you want when you're having sex. You can only know his gestures are sincere after you've been with him for a long time. Intimacy makes many men feel vulnerable. And heaven forbid they feel this way! Many guys shut it off when out of the heat of passion. Passion means getting carried away, which can translate to a loss of control, so many guys are silent during sex. It's easier to focus on being tender than to risk losing control in bed. That's why we'll keep reminding you—your chance of a good relationship is better if you wait to sleep with him. Says David:

" Remember that when you're in bed with someone, you really should care about him. If not, it will be pretty meaningless. Not that casual sex doesn't have a use. It does. It keeps us from making stupid decisions and getting involved quickly with the wrong people. But if you're going to work on an intimate sexual relationship, it should be with somebody whom you respect and care about. Most human beings are wired in that the more they care about each other, the better the sex is, and the fuller the experience they're going to have. **99**

Keep His Hat On!

Guys who practice unsafe sex are dangerous. Many men try to convince a new partner to skip the condoms. MANY! And too many women succumb to the pressure and manipulation given to avoid using them as they attempt to please. A man can lay on a serious guilt trip if his southern head is cheering him on and our desire to keep him happy makes us succumb. A large percentage of men prefer not using those rubbery covers over their manhoods. Ed says it takes away from sexual pleasure:

66 Men don't want to wear condoms for various reasons, the most predominant ones being that it seems unnatural, is uncomfortable, and tends to ruin the moment if you're in a very passionate situation. To stop and suit up can kill the FANTASY part of the sexual act, especially if it is spontaneous. But you shouldn't skip condoms. It all comes back to SELF-WORTH. If you don't value yourself enough to insist on using them, then why should he? Not to mention diseases, pregnancy, etc. **99**

"Sex shouldn't be a game of Russian roulette. Think of the penis as a present—it's always better when wrapped."   —Randall

Gay guys respect safe sex a lot more than straight ones. Straight men complain that they lose their erections with a condom. The guys say that's a crock! He can be turned on and distracted for long enough to slip it on. Men don't like to think of their "nice" women as people who'd catch a disease. But—that's how they get spread! Nice people carry diseases too. They get it from other nice people who felt condoms weren't necessary, who got it from other nice people who felt condoms weren't necessary.

Do you get the drift? No one is immune based on class or what type of person they are. Protect yourself, no matter what he says! Straight men think they're invincible. "It can't happen to me." Sorry, but anybody can catch a long list of diseases. Carl agrees:

66 Men don't want condoms because it feels better without them. This is probably the most politically incorrect thing I could possibly say, but it's true. Yet life is full of tradeoffs, and in this case the tradeoff is literally life—yours, his, and possibly an unwanted child's. So you need to be confident in yourself and respectful of your own life. That means that you insist—always—on safety. You don't buy stupid lines like 'I'm clean' or 'I've only been with quality people.' Be prepared; don't count on anyone else to bring the protection. He should, but you should be ready in case he doesn't. If you educate yourself about the risks and how to minimize them, you'll have less to worry about and can focus on the good stuff. 99

Statistics show that sexually transmitted diseases (STDs) are spreading faster than guys can make excuses for not using condoms. That's why you must use them and keep using them until you and your guy get tested for HIV and other STDs because you plan to be together for a while. Even then, go with him for his test and the results. The guys say men will lie about that too! Kyle warns:

66 I tell my girlfriends that having sex without a condom is like having sex with every person that man has been with. Since men can be sluts—you certainly don't know where they've been. 99

"If a guy insists on not wearing a condom—DUMP THE BAS-TARD! A man who doesn't value you is a jerk!"   —Kenny

Don't fall for excuses men give you. His pleasure ain't as important as your life. The guys and I know that. It's time for you to accept it too. Horny guys can be very convincing. They know how to make you feel guilty if his southern head goes soft. Don't go soft in your head! Erections can be brought back to attention once he knows his choice is a condom or no nookie. We're saying a bit about this topic because it's so important for you to accept it. When you're in the heat of a sexual moment and he's pouring on the romance, no woman likes to feel like she's ruining it by refusing to continue unless he covers up. But you must insist, no matter how convincing he is, explains Michael M.:

❝ You should never put your life at risk for anybody, no matter if they're gonna lose their erection. HE needs to learn how to keep his erection with a condom. That's a copout for a lot of guys who want to have sex without one. It doesn't feel as stimulating. Guys may say that to a woman to manipulate her. Living in this age, your life needs to be your number-one concern—before anything. If someone is telling you they don't want to use a condom, you need to walk away from him. Five minutes isn't worth a life of pain and disease. ❞

Learn to put the condom on. Start by unrolling the top a tad so you can see which way it goes on. Tell him to lay back and enjoy. Then distract him with enough pleasure that he doesn't notice the condom being slipped on.

Putting the condom on while stimulating him does work. Catch him unaware. Go down on him. Suck him. Get him worked up. Men lose their senses from oral sex. Open the condom package before-hand. As you get him off guard with oral sex, slip it out of the package. When he's lost in what you're doing, gently slide the rubber down his shaft. Ready for intercourse! If necessary, practice putting a condom on a cucumber to get good at it. If he still balks about safe sex, play it safe by just using your hands or not having any sex. He may get used to condoms if you refuse to give in. Michele adds:

❝ I'm sorry, but I cannot call a guy who doesn't want to wear condoms 'a man.' No excuses! There are plenty of sexually trans-mitted infections. Furthermore, a woman must think of children, too!

I am very intolerant about this! I've always used condoms with all my partners, as something natural. It's respect for each other and simple—no condoms, no sex completely. You can help him. Put it on for him. Keep on touching him, masturbating him till he's ready. Try new positions. Lick him all around the penis area to help him to wear this 'delicate glove,' and I'm sure it's going to stay hard! **"**

"Any man worth your time of day will respect your efforts to protect yourself and him."   —Yiannis

Romance a la Testosterone

My favorite boyfriend (whom I'll call Tom) was also my most unromantic—by female standards. He brought flowers the first day we made love—and never again, despite my many complaints. Tom didn't get it. "Don't I bring you cut-up watermelon?" He was pleased with himself about that! I wasn't. When I was sick he cooked for me. He cut out articles he knew I'd like, showing he paid attention to my interests. And he did many other very considerate things that showed he cared. But I still wanted flowers! A guy's concept of romance can be very different from a woman's. Fritz wants you to appreciate what a guy does in the name of romance:

" Guys don't do what girls want—like giving a hug or kiss. They show their affection in different ways than women want to see. Guys will do things to protect you and make you feel safer. But it might not be what you want. He's not going to say he cares about you. He's going to do it with an action. Your car might get washed. 🗩🗩

"I do think men can be taught. It's more like monkey see, monkey do. They can imitate it. I don't know if they can learn it." —Rick

Tom's actions screamed "I care about you!" And I appreciated them greatly. But, like most girls, I still wanted the flowers and other overt romantic gestures, no matter how evolved I am. Romance makes us feel good, because films and TV teach us it's what guys should do. Why shouldn't I get that? Vinnie explains:

🗩🗩 We all have some notion of the course of relationships and what our roles are supposed to be. Movies teach us what romance and courting should be like. I don't think real life is anything like that. You shouldn't have unrealistic expectations. Sex is a guy's version of romance. I want to believe that romance does exist, but it's in a way that's different than we see in movies. Think about this. We don't even kiss like they do in movies. Have you tried to make a kiss look like it does in movies? We don't look like that. 🗩🗩

Men don't pay attention to romantic movies or seek to emulate them, as we'd like them to. Being more practical, they show caring by doing nice things. I had NO doubt how Tom felt about me. But despite my protests, he remained intractable about giving me compliments, romantic gestures, flowers, and verbal expressions of his feelings. Grrrr. . . . Yet he showed love in much more sincere ways than words. Kevin K. reminded me:

❝ What men really desire the most is the opportunity to give their love and have it appreciated. But for this to happen women must come to appreciate that the language of love men speak is often different from their own. They don't want so much to talk of love as to demonstrate it. Given ample opportunity men use that language fluently and graciously. I've noticed that many women receiving eloquent love letters from their men miss the message because they don't understand the language. ❞

Better communication—with details about why you need a girl's version of romance—might be more productive than whining in generalities. You must explain how good you feel when you get compliments or why flowers are a symbol of caring. We expect men to know this stuff and get mad if one doesn't satisfy the need for romance a la female. Guys get frustrated after doing what they think is a lot and getting only a lack of appreciation and complaints. There is a way around this, advises Fritz:

❝ A lot of it comes down to good communication skills. Start by complimenting the things about him you like, and don't bring up what you didn't like. Guys love to get praised as much as anyone. If he knows he's going in the right direction, he'll repeat that behavior again. ❞

"An attempt—whether feigned or not—to show an interest in his hobbies and pursuits might just do the trick."   —Patrick

Pavlov's dogs got it, and guys can too. Repetitive behavior, followed by rewards when he gets it, trains him to give you more of what you want. He needs to experience how romance can enhance sex. That's what's on his brain. Show by example what you like. When he does something romantic, however small, and he gets a good response, especially if it's oral sex, he's more likely to try harder next time.

"Turn him on with romance when he least expects it. Don't just give him roses. Leave them in a trail strewn through the house, and have the last one be on your naked body. Love is deeper by the dozen that way."   —Mike

Be romantic and loving to your guy. Compliment him. Guys don't get as many compliments as we do, and most really lap them up with pleasure. Tell him he has a sexy butt. Let him know how good he makes you feel. Guys love to hear that you think they're strong, sexy, capable, a stud in bed, and anything else that you feel.

Don't lie. If there aren't things to compliment, why are you with him? He may understand better when he sees how great romance makes him feel if you give him a good taste of what you'd like to receive. David recommends:

❝ Be romantic first. Tell him you want to spend some quality time and that you've drawn a warm, wonderful bath. Turn off the lights, put on a bunch of candles and some music. Don't make the bath too fruity or flowery. Use a musky scent, something sexy and spicy because you'll have a man in that tub, too. Most men will do it. Or take a picnic basket and go somewhere. Bring a blanket, and some condoms, too—just in case it gets really good. Never pass up a moment to bang it out where you need to do it. Be spontaneous. Take whatever direction you think your guy might be into and elaborate on it. ❞

"I think every man has a different level of romanticism that he's comfortable with. You sort of get what you get in this area."

—Ed

Your guy might just not want to be romantic, no matter how much it means to you. That tells you something on a broader level about who he is. His lack of romance can tell you other things about him. It may reflect a lack of passion for life in general. Or he may not care enough. You deserve a guy who wants to give you what you need, as long as it's not unreasonable. There are plenty of men who are romantic or who will at least give it a shot.

"Give him an unforgettable moment of romance. And, if he doesn't understand, move over—there are a lot of nice guys out there."   —Michele

How can you show him romance? Decide how important romance is to you. Be realistic in what you expect. Whenever he does something romantic, even if it's by accident, make a fuss and let him know how much you like it. Give him better sex when he's romantic beforehand. That might spur him. Patience and compliments are the best way to draw romance out of him.

First-Aid Tips

- When you're seeing someone, ALWAYS have condoms with you. Not having one is NOT a good excuse for unsafe sex.
- Try something new to please yourself sexually.
- Explore online sex stores (www.goodvibes.com, www.babeland.com, www.evesgarden.com, etc.).

THE REAL RULES ABOUT MEN

New Directions That Empower You

*"I think men play the same games, but
women are a little more adept at them."*

—Brian

Many women join forces with friends to create rules about how
to behave with men. Some books state actual rules about what we
should and shouldn't do to control them. They say if you do "this,"
he'll love you more. Do "that," and he'll do things your way. Most
of the guys and I believe these types of rules hurt self-esteem by
putting too much emphasis on what pleases a guy and not enough
on you. Why make men so important that we follow rules of behavior to get and keep one?

Those kinds of rules can make you feel that men are more valuable than you! Besides, following them attracts guys who love a
chase but run when your guard goes down. Why not know from the
get-go if he likes the real you? How long can you keep up the façade?
Will you play games for the duration of the relationship?

"Playing games will backfire on you. Someone always gets hurt."

—Glenn

When you have a satisfying life, you don't have to follow rules to prove to a guy that you can live without him. He sees it! I asked the guys to suggest some more empowering rules that can guide you to be a healthy partner in a relationship. These rules support a satisfying life by focusing on YOU, not him.

RULE #1: Declare Independence from Rules, Games, and Stereotypes!

The kind of rules advocated in books can lower self-esteem by inferring that men won't like or respect you without them, which is wrong! Rules give men more importance than we give ourselves. If a guy doesn't behave properly, following rules won't change him for real. You've got to develop enough self-confidence to keep you from feeling a need to play those kinds of games, according to Dan. But as Jason points out, our upbringing begins the process:

❝ Women have all these rules growing up about how they are supposed to be and how they are supposed to act. They're supposed to wait to be asked out and they're not supposed to have sex. They're supposed to want a man to take care of them. ❞

Rules that focus on him direct you to put more thought and energy into HIS needs. Your real power is in controlling YOU! That enables you to send the best message without trying so hard. Why not go after a guy who respects you for real? Men get cues on how to treat you from how they see you treat yourself. Having a full, satisfying life on your own generates the same results as following rules, but in a healthier way. And it's a lot more fun! You won't seem dependent if you have a full life that doesn't revolve around him. Kevin K. urges:

> **"** Forget the rules! By their nature, rules harness and restrict human effort. Instead, flourish through imagination, intuition, and appreciation. Blossom, don't restrict. When I studied massage, our instructor told us we would give our best massages when we forgot everything he taught us and instead just let the massage flow through us. He was right. The same goes with many things in life, because when we engage in such unself-conscious forgetfulness, we let life flow through us. We can then trust the outcome. I wonder how many opportunities for glorious relationships we throw away because of the tension we create by trying to get it right. **"**

The rationales behind some of the rules make sense. You shouldn't give yourself away to anyone. But taking care of yourself should be a lifestyle, not a rule you follow. If you feel good about you, you won't need to prove yourself. You're living the good vibe!

Do you want to be in a real relationship? Then be real! Otherwise, what's your prize? A guy who you manipulated? Do you really think that sets the tone for a trusting relationship? We don't. There is a big difference between playing games and handling yourself in a way that reflects your independence. A truly independent lifestyle, not one created by games, will get the results you want in a more satisfying, honest way.

RULE #2: Make YOU #1!

What part of numero uno don't you understand? That should be YOUR number, not his! We treat men like kings, catering to their needs and putting aside our interests and friends to be there for them. If you want a guy who treats you well, put your needs first. That's not selfish. It's healthy for you, which ultimately benefits others.

When you're happy, you have more to give others because you want to, not to win them over. If you make yourself less important than your guy is, he will too. And why shouldn't he take if you're giving freely? Straight guys can be a bit self-absorbed on their own. Don't reinforce it! Rick advises:

> **66** You should never make him more important than you. Never. If you're worrying about what he's going to think or when he's going to call, that's a big bore. You're the prize, not him. You have to look at it that way. **99**

> "You deserve to be treated like a queen—or at least be complimented by one. Keep a gay man on hand for self-esteem emergencies."
> —Randy

Following rules meant to attract and keep a guy will magnify his importance. Magnify your own instead! Exuding a positive self-image is way hotter than being a woman who tries too hard. Confidence and an attitude that shows self-value are attractive and keep him on his toes better than rules do. Fritz suggests:

66 Make yourself feel important. There's nothing more attractive to anyone than confidence. If you make yourself feel important, people are going to pick up on that. You can compare it to 'dress for success.' If you dress the part, you feel the part. People will go toward you if you come across as a powerful person with confidence. 99

RULE #3: Be Yourself

If you act as the woman you want to be, not as the woman you think a guy wants, the right man will want the woman you are. Following rules is putting on an act. Why would you want to be with a guy who falls for someone you're really not?

> "Don't become the person you think they want you to be. It will be an awfully long life if you're acting out something that you don't feel true to."   —Fritz

The trouble is, many of us don't know ourselves well if we've been playing a chameleon to the whims of each guy we date. It can take time, therapy, and a break from immersion in a relationship. When you work on yourself from the inside out, you get to know you. That gives you an opportunity to discover a person you like. Then you can drop the rules and be yourself. Michael McD. explains:

> 66 I think rules are game playing, which is what you should not do. The best thing you can do is be yourself. There's always a little bit of game playing in the beginning. But if someone's interested, they're interested. You don't need to play games. Being honest is the best thing to do. You'll attract more people who are emotionally available when you yourself are more emotionally available. 99

> "Rules imply there's a game being played. Just be YOU! Of course that requires that you take the time to know who YOU are first!"   —Ed

As you develop a life apart from having a romantic partner, it's easier to be yourself in any situation. Being yourself can be hard to do. Even confident people have moments of concern about how they'll be judged. We do live in a judgmental society. But when we're not counting on HIM for a life, there's less at stake when you stop the games. You can start dropping the rules slowly as you work on strengthening yourself and putting it out. Kyle sees a lot more merit in being the real you:

❝ The best way to attract a healthy relationship is by being honest from the get-go. My friend Andrea wanted to impress this guy and felt she had to act differently around him than she was around her friends. They had a more than tumultuous relationship for over a year. Since she had to keep up her act, it put a strain on her. When his true colors showed, the relationship turned into a constant battle. It caused her a lot of grief that could have been avoided. She is not my only friend who made this mistake. **❞**

We don't advocate letting everything hang out quickly. Let him get to know you slowly. Parcel out what you share. If you're super-independent, don't overdo it on the first few dates. Give him tastes of who you are as a person. As you get more involved, more aspects can become evident.

RULE #4: Value Your Space—and His

Guys balk when they feel smothered. Yet many women have a strong need to be with their guys as much as possible, which creates static. When you can enjoy time apart, consider yourself whole. A healthy relationship thrives on being able to nurture your own space and respect his right to have his. Michael A. says:

❝ Giving each other space allows some breathing and lets fresh air into the room. It allows you to have new experiences with a partner you've been with for a long time. **❞**

"Guys hate to be smothered. They can sense it coming on from a mile away."   —Andy

When you have a life apart from him and genuine enthusiasm for doing things solo or with friends, it keeps him on his toes. He knows you're a chick with a life, with or without him. While guys complain about clingy women, they're more secure with them.

Many women go ballistic when their guys want space. If you act happy to have time for other things, enjoy his confusion. Getting upset about his plans that don't involve you makes him secure that you'll always be there for him. An independent woman won't stay if he isn't good to her. Your acceptance can make him uneasy, without playing a game. His need for time without you is normal, so make your own plans. Relax and enjoy your space! It's usually unnecessary to worry when a partner wants his own space. Different people need different amounts of space, explains Michael McD.:

66 If someone tells you he needs space, listen and try as much as possible not to take it personally. The worst thing to do is take stuff like that personally. You might think, 'He doesn't want to be with me,' when it has nothing to do with you. It's hard to believe at the time—in the moment. Some people require more space than others. Some just need more personal time. When you try to infringe on someone's space, they'll run away quicker. Don't smother him. 99

RULE #5: Don't Say You're Busy—*Be* Busy!

A well-known rule is to say you're busy if a guy calls after Wednesday. Even if you have nothing to do and want to see him, you're encouraged to sit home, probably sulking, rather than accept a date because he called "too late." Why? You don't want him thinking that you're desperate by accepting an invitation at the last minute.

That rationale works for those with low self-esteem. A confident woman knows that what she thinks of herself matters most. If you feel good about who you are, why worry about what he thinks in situations like that? Carl explains:

66 You can accept the late invite, but don't change other plans to do so. Don't dump your night out with the girls just because Johnny Come Lately finally figures out how to use the telephone. If you have to turn down the date, but you really like the guy, just say so. Make a counterproposal: 'Wow, I'd really love to see you again, but I already have plans for Saturday night that I can't break. Could we get together later this week for dinner or a movie?' 99

"If you're both playing games, that's all the relationship will ever be—a game."   —Alex

Instead of saying that you're busy, BE BUSY! A girl with a life doesn't sit around waiting for his call. She makes her own plans if he doesn't ask her out early in the week. And when he finally asks, she doesn't break plans to accept the date. Canceling plans with friends to be with him is the no-no—a rule all women should follow. Being busy helps him think twice about calling too late. Plus, it's more pleasant than turning his offer down just to give him a message.

Being busy for real—and not canceling plans with friends just to see him—gets the message across without complaining that he calls too late. Meanwhile, you'll have more fun. Let him wonder what you're up to! Rick learned early that sending a subtle message by being busy is good:

    ❝ Years ago, my mother sat me and my sisters down at the kitchen table and said there's nothing wrong with any relationship with a little cat-and-mouse. I think that being a little unavailable is good in a relationship. **❞**

That said, if a guy you like calls after Wednesday and you're free, accept the date if you want to go. If he does it regularly, make other plans more often. This feels more empowering than lying and missing out on fun. Patrick advises:

    ❝ If you want to go out on the date, go. Just because a man is calling you at the last minute and you accept doesn't mean you are desperate or that your chassis will be perceived as the last lemon on the lot. Men are generally forgetful and leave the business of procuring a date until the last minute. **❞**

When you feel confident in yourself, don't worry that he'll judge you. What's more important is what you think of you. If you plan a solo day and he calls, that's being busy too. I always smile when I tell a guy I already have plans when it's something I'm doing for me. There's always another day, and it's lovely to value my own time. But accept if you're free and want to go out. Life is too short to play games, and give up something you'd enjoy, just to prove a point. Yiannis sets you straight about making choices that will bring you the most pleasure:

> " If your focus in the relationship is playing games, you'll definitely want to put your man off if he calls too late in the week. If your focus is spending time with somebody who you find attractive, intelligent, and witty, get off your high horse and go on the date. "

You can point out that you have a lot going on, he's lucky you were free, and you'd prefer him to call earlier in the week. Don't make a fuss about it. There are better ways to get your message across—like being busy for real. Alex explains:

> " Is the fact that he called late in the week for a date all that's important? If it bothers you that much, be honest about it without being confrontational. That could mean the difference between a late date and no date. "

Often it's what you don't say that tells him the most. You don't have to share everything you do and who you see. Women feel they have to go into details about everything, while guys give us the barest facts. Emulate him when he inquires about your plans, by being vague while smiling sweetly. If he calls when you're not home and asks where you were, just say "Out." A game? No? You were out! You can give the minimum answers to his questions—without lying, if he doesn't tell you all his details. It will help to prevent him from taking you for granted. Don't make not telling him stuff a game, but there's no need to share every little detail like many of us do. You're entitled to some privacy.

RULE #6: Call Him If You Want To

Let common sense, not rules, dictate whether you call him. Do what suits you—good self-esteem allows you not to worry about what he'll think about your actions. Vinnie explains:

66 I know one of those rules is that you don't call him. That's such bullshit! I think you should put out on the first date. I'm serious. I've played that myself—trying to play hard to get—wait until Wednesday. I don't believe in that. People don't call back. There's no guarantee of a second date no matter what you do 99

"Sure, why not call? Just don't become a stalker, and make sure if he has caller ID that you don't do that call and hang-up thing just to see if he's home when he said he will be! Damn technology!"

—Ed

If you feel like calling a guy, call. You may not feel like it, but follow your instincts. If it's meant to be with him, says Yiannis, it will work out whether you call or not:

> 66 It all depends on what type of man you're trying to attract. If you're looking for some meathead who thinks that appropriate courting etiquette involves a large club and a dark cave, definitely do not call—it will seem too aggressive. If you're looking to attract the type of man who respects a woman who controls her own destiny and pursues what she wants with a passion, start dialing. 99

Limit your calls if you're not comfortable. But if you feel like calling, do it. It won't change the opinion of a guy who is interested. And if he's not, you might find out faster. Once you're seeing someone, make calling him natural. Jason shares advice he gives to his mother, who is now single:

> 66 Women still feel that they have to wait for men to call them. I say to my mother, 'If you like someone, you pick him.' I think straight men like to be found and don't like to always have to make the first move. 99

Just don't call constantly or enough times to make you uncomfortable if there's no reciprocation. And don't hold him hostage on the phone by yakking nonstop. Most guys don't call so much because they don't like talking on the phone. So don't add to his aversion to phone chatting by making it last too long. Otherwise, guys do like to hear from a woman they like. Bob emphatically encourages you not to let rules prevent you from calling him if you want to:

> 66 Yes, yes, yes, yes, yes. And yes. Men fancy themselves as mountains—but mostly of insecurities, self-doubts, and anxieties. They have no instincts about what makes them attractive to anyone else, so they have no clue whether a woman will respond to them at all. You can almost feel the sigh of relief when a guy realizes that a self-confident, interesting woman who has something to say is willing to take the first step! 99

Rule #7: Live for Today

Enjoy your life now! Stop worrying so much about long-term commitments. That's how guys live, and we can learn this from them. Following this rule helps you milk more joy out of each day. Live for the moment, advises Michael A.:

> 66 Living in the moment helps you not have as much worry. You'll be well rested. The moment is the only thing that lives in you. For me, it happens when I'm playing tennis or sports. There is nothing but the ball and the racket. When you live in the moment you're a part of something greater. 99

> "Learn to live more in the moment instead of looking toward the future, or you'll only worry all the more."   —Mike

We often dilute pleasure by projecting into the future or drive ourselves nuts by rehashing things that happened. That creates worries that aren't necessary. Just because HE promises you the stars, the moon, and the sun doesn't mean you get anything more than words from him.

You can make all sorts of plans for getting married and being together. But until the future comes, it's all speculation. Allow the future to get here when it comes. Meanwhile, enjoy today. Right now really is all that matters because it's the only thing you're experiencing. Learn from guys and live more in the now. Michael McD. explains:

> **"** Girls think more of the future and the past. Guys are more in the moment and probably lose sight of the future and past at times. Live in the moment too! Forget about the future and learn from the past. Just enjoy the ride. It is a journey, and you should enjoy and appreciate it while it lasts. **"**

RULE #8: Take Risks

Don't be afraid to try new things. Go after something you might be afraid of. Date men who might not meet all your rigid criteria if they seem like decent people. You never know who you might meet if you don't take risks, Michael A. points out:

> **"** You have a lot to gain by taking risks. Women lead much richer emotional lives than men. Because you're in touch with your

feelings more and have a much greater sense of what you like, need, and don't like, it behooves you to take the kind of risks that will give you the rewards of those capacities. **"**

Taking risks builds confidence and keep, life more interesting. If you meet a guy who seems special, go for it, no matter what others say. You only have one life, and staying in the safe lane keeps you safe but can be boring. Go after a guy who seems like someone who could rock your world. Not a bad boy but just someone who's different than the type you usually date. Let him know you're interested. The worst that can happen is that you find out that he isn't. Bob emphatically says:

" Falling in love is a crapshoot, and staying in love is joy and effort. But finding someone you think is worth your attention is really taking chances each and every single day so that you don't live with any doubts, regrets, and lost opportunities. There are millions of people who want to connect with each other; and too many let all the inner and outer voices tell them they can't, they shouldn't, and they mustn't. So, just go for it and see what happens. Taking a chance is the number-one rule for making your own path in life. If you wait for someone else to take a chance, you will be on the sidelines for too long. **"**

RULE #9: Expect to Be Treated Well

If you expect a guy to treat you well, there's a better chance he will treat you in more satisfying ways. If he doesn't, leave. Period. No excuses or extra chances. No settling for less than good. If you treat yourself well and expect good behavior from your guy, it will come across to him. Jerks who ignore the message need to be sent off. If you act like you have no value, he won't value you! Matthew explains:

66 It's like Psych 101. I see a lot of straight women almost offering themselves as doormats. When you so eagerly volunteer your own power to anyone else, it devalues you. Even if men don't consciously realize it, they subconsciously see you as a devalued product, for lack of a better concept. It really bothers me to see that. 99

When a guy knows how you expect to be treated, he'll do so if he really likes you. If you send him packing, he may return with a new attitude. Set boundaries right from the start so you don't have to change your expectations later when he's used to getting away with bad behavior. But even if you've cut him too much slack, you can pull in the reins and stop the drama. A man who wants you can be trained by your response to unacceptable behavior. Mike advises:

66 Be more assertive about what you want in the relationship. I would like to think by now that women don't have to put their needs above those of their men, but we know not all women have broken out of that thought cycle. All women and all men should expect to be treated well. Didn't Madonna say, 'Don't go for second best . . . put your love to the test'? It's advice for all women, not just glamorous blondes. 99

"You don't get what you want. You get what you expect."

—Michael A.

First-Aid Tips

- Put up Post-it notes with positive thoughts about yourself, such as "I'm a very special woman"; "I'm terrific the way I am"; "Any man who's with me is lucky"; and so on. Whenever you look at one, read it out loud.
- Write down old beliefs about how you're supposed to behave with a man and think about how it will feel to let go of those old rules.
- Buy something that adds a special touch to your living space, to increase your pleasure when you're home.

Make Him a Keeper

Tips for Nurturing Good Behavior in Your Guy

"You have to be very willing to get to know somebody."
—*Jason*

I truly believe that one woman's jerk can be another woman's treasure. It's all a matter of how you handle YOURSELF from the beginning. A guy is more likely to take advantage of you if he knows you're desperate for someone. When you have a life that he has to compete with, you're in the driver's seat. In this chapter we give you tips for creating treasures. Pay attention to how men date. They sure have more fun than many of us! Kyle explains:

> 66 Women can learn how to date from men. Most men don't take it as seriously as women do. You can't go on dates or get into a relationship planning on it being the 'big' one. Go on dates and find out what kind of people you like, and learn from it. And don't obsess! 99

Friendly Nookie

Did you ever jump into a relationship because of intense chemistry, before developing the friendship side of your interaction? That can sabotage the potential for a relationship. If you've been without a guy and are craving one who rocks your world, you might dive in fast when you find one.

Diving in can mean sexually, but it can be emotionally too—confiding too much, seeing him too often, expressing feelings, and trusting him too quickly. It can unravel fast once the initial glow calms down. Eventually his flaws come out and aggravate you. If they're big, even the glow of good sex won't replace the friendship you never developed with him. Friends discuss what's bothering them to work out problems. When you go fast, there's often no time to get to know each other as friends. It's hard for a relationship to be healthy without friendship as a foundation, says Alex:

66 Somebody that you intend to spend the rest of your life with, ideally, should be your closest friend. If you don't have that friendship, then your relationship is based on something very insubstantial, very thin, and problems will show up later on. If your partner is also your friend, when the kinks come, and they will come, you can straighten them out. 99

"If you can't be friends with your partners, then you will never find a true balance of sexual and emotional intimacy."   —Kyle

After a breakup, many couples wonder why they're not still friends. Because they were never friends to begin with! You can't remain friends after a breakup if you didn't have the foundation of friendship before. When it's all about sex, there's nothing without physical contact. Don't let the ecstasy of romance allow you to forget how important real friendship is, unless you're just with him for a short-term fling. Rick explains:

> 66 It's really hard to set boundaries at first because you just want to go for it, have lots of sex, and have fun. You never think about boundaries because you don't want to put boundaries on your sex life. You want to do everything. But if you're friends in the beginning and get to know his personality, you might have a better indicator of what he might be capable of that would piss you off in the future. 99

When your boyfriend/lover/husband is also your good friend, it's easier to deal with problems. Communication also works better when you have a strong foundation of friendship. Curt explains some benefits:

> 66 It's better to be friends first because you discover the person's faults and don't have to break up with him. You decide if you can handle that factor in a relationship. You make an assessment if he's someone you want to be with. 99

Friendship is a key element that's missing in many relationships that have major problems. When you jump into intimacy fast, it's harder to develop a strong foundation for other things. Friendship is often the concrete that holds it all together. It enables you to build a solid level of trust and creates a comfortable connection that can withstand a lot.

When you get intense early, it can also be more difficult to become friends. Try to go slow with a guy you might get involved with and get to know him as a person first to see if friendship can develop. If he's someone you can't be friends with, a healthy relationship won't evolve. Real friendship can't begin until you're being yourself, and if you wait too long it may be too late, says Kyle:

> 66 With dating, there is almost always a level of acting involved. Both people want to impress the other, and so they may pretend to be a certain way or try to give off a certain vibe. After a little while, though, you begin to see the real person, and it may very well be someone whom you don't like. If two people get to know each other by beginning with a much more raw and honest relationship, this problem can be easily avoided. 99

> "If you really are good friends, you're able to laugh together. Without that, you've got nothing."   —Rick

We highly advise you to become friends with any man you want intimacy with so that you can know him on many levels. If you can't get the friendship going, beware! Jerks don't make good friends. Be VERY wary if a guy isn't friendship material—he may just be good for in the sack. But making love to a guy who's also your friend can result in the best sex! Randall adds:

66 Relationships are hard. Really challenging. So few couples are actually going to make it for a long haul, but if a friendship is established first, chances are you'll have another worthwhile friend if or when the romance fades away. 99

Keep Him Guessing—Just a Little

First impressions last. They can set a tone for future encounters with a guy you've just met. When you try too hard to impress a guy you're attracted to and let him get away with unacceptable behavior before you've gotten to know each other, you may later regret it. If you have a great life to fall back on, it's easier to date consciously and stay cool while you heat up inside.

Since it's better to take your time getting to know a guy, control yourself and your feelings until you've had plenty of time to gauge what kind of guy he really is. Michael M. advises:

66 I do recommend a little game playing at the beginning of a relationship. I think initially you have to play hard to get. Once you're in a relationship, though, you have to stop game playing. Only do it for the courting process. 99

"I always tell my women friends not to be too easy. It's good to have a little space between longing and desire."   —Brian

Holding back at the beginning is not necessarily game playing. It's maintaining control over your actions and tending to your life. Stay busy after you fall for him. There's less time to analyze, and he won't take it for granted that you're waiting for his call. It's healthy to put reins on premature feelings that can get out of control if you immerse yourself in him. Let the relationship develop one step at a time. Travis admits:

66 I hate to say it, but play a little hard to get. I swear it must go back to our hunting days when we lived in caves—men love the chase, and they can fall in love with you while they pursue you. Don't be a tease when it comes to sex or lead the guy on. Just give him enough room to know you are interested and give him a chance to show he is interested in you. Then you will have him hooked. 99

Don't play hard to get—be hard to get because you have other things in your life! If you meet someone you like, go on with your life. Don't start revolving around him. If you REALLY like him, stay very busy so you can stay out of trouble. Matthew suggests:

66 Hold back more. You don't like to do that because you think you'll lose him. But holding back makes guys come toward you more. The past generation had that figured out. They didn't jump

into bed on the first date—in the sexual sense, but also in the sense of giving everything from the word *go*. When women draw their own boundaries and own their power, men learn to respect them. **"**

Those special connections that develop instantly make us want to jump in fast. But often one party can't handle it—usually him. Remember, many men are hit-and-run daters. They fall hard for something about you that they need and dive in fast. Don't follow. Put on the brakes if he pushes to see you all the time, even if you have to get a friend to tie you up. Don't get caught up in a dating accident. Men that come on like a speeding car will crash faster than others do. If you want it to last, slow him down, no matter how good it feels. Michael M. explains:

" When you start pushing a relationship in the early stages, it shows that you're too desperate. It scares people. You have to get to know each other. Give it time. You can't force falling in love. It's great to go slow because that way you get to know each other. **"**

Guys scare themselves when they get carried away and push you to move fast. As soon as you join the race and it gets good, he may feel trapped and disappear. If you want to have a relationship instead of a passionate, fast-paced fling, don't take his words and insistence seriously. Humor him instead of hanging onto his words in excitement. Make plans with other people so you can't see him constantly. Control YOU, and you control the pace. Jason adds:

" If you want to have sex, you find guys to have sex with and you never see them again. If you want a relationship, those are the guys you date slowly. Don't mix it up. "

However, going to any extreme isn't good. Playing too hard to get can also backfire on you. While you don't want to fall all over your new guy, let him know you're interested. If you don't make him too important, it's easier to get on with your life and take dating one day at a time instead of projecting into the future and planning for what you hope will happen with him (which probably won't become a reality). Patrick provides some instructions:

" How to handle yourself when first meeting a guy:

1. Start by being charming, yet distracted by more important matters.
2. Then give a smile that displays subtle intrigue or amusement toward the guy.
3. Move to outright flirtation and sexual innuendo.

If you're not likely to see this man again, don't dillydally—the steps should proceed in convincing, thirty-second to one-minute intervals. For a coworker, friend of a friend, neighbor, or UPS deliveryman, provided he's not gay, the steps can be drawn out for a week at a time. "

Get a good balance between being indifferent and enjoying the fun of meeting a guy who turns you on. If you like a guy, let it show, at least somewhat. Don't try to stifle all your feelings. Dan believes:

66 Part of the fun of being in relationships, dating, or romance is your natural, chemical response to being excited about someone. That kind of excitement is very attractive. It's better to go a little overboard than to hide your feelings or be too cool. Aloof is boring. 99

"Flirt when you meet a guy you like."   —Andy

Just don't dive in without a life preserver—common sense or strong friends with common sense. Being flirtatious is fun, and guys like it. There's a difference between light, teasing flirtation and sexual innuendoes. Keep it light, and let him wonder how much you like him.

Start with a Little Mystery

Don't tell your entire dating history on the first date. Make a good impression by not talking way too much. Small talk works better for getting to know each other in small bits. If it turns into a relationship, you'll have plenty of time to fill him in on your life. A bit of mystery is sexy, points out Brian:

66 Women should retain a sense of their own mystery. I think women tend to reveal too many things at once, when they just start

dating. They should pace what they want men to know about them and shouldn't tell everything on the first date. I used to be that way. **99**

> "Mystery leaves him something to find, and what fun the looking part can be!"   —Mike

Watch his attitude about other women in his life, like his mom. If he speaks negatively about former girlfriends, a red light should come on. Men who still think well of them are more likely to treat you well later. Glenn recommends:

66 Ask questions. Find out about him, and go slow. Evaluate your life and what you want. Write down the dos and don'ts so you know what to look for. **99**

Avoid negative topics—how badly you've been hurt in the past. That makes some men wonder about you. Plus, they hate hearing it. Stay in the now as much as possible. Bitterness toward ex-boyfriends is a sign to your current guy that you carry grudges or have issues. Fritz says:

66 I get this from a lot of clients who are guys. They complain that their women trash their ex-boyfriends—spend a whole day talking about that. Girls don't like when a guy does that either. You're not with your ex. You're looking for a future, something new. Focus on that. **99**

"Men see women as a mystery and are intrigued by it. They want to be intrigued and pulled into you, so to speak. That turns men on." —Matthew

Don't try to book all his time. Guys like a woman who respects his need for space, and who enjoys her own. Never stop trying to pace yourself SLOWLY. It's fun to get all mushy with someone you're falling for and discuss plans for the next year. Stifle that course! You don't know him well enough to plan more than your next date. Don't tell him about the tickets you're getting for a show in two months or your friend's upcoming wedding. If he's still in your picture when it's a week away, invite him.

Long-term plans can scare him in the beginning. And they're not appropriate until you know him VERY well! Men don't like commitments, Jason says. Get to know him better first:

66 No one wants to feel crowded at first. You have to find out what each person's like because everyone is different. People's perceptions are different. You have to ask a lot of questions when you're on a date with somebody. 99

Dress to Impress

Think about how you want to look for your first date. Wear something you feel good in and that reflects who you are. But don't stress over it. Men sure don't go to that kind of trouble for a date! Kenny advises:

66 Don't think about it too much at all. Choose something to wear as if you were meeting a good friend. Once you start dressing to impress a guy, it's already starting out in an unhealthy way. 99

"You can either dress because you want to turn him on or because you want to feel good about yourself. Do you want to be the girl that he shags and then dumps or the one he takes home to Mom?"
　　　　　　　　　　　　　　　　　　　—Fritz

Being a little low-key seems to be the style of choice. Some of the guys suggest being a little provocative without going overboard. Carl explains some basics:

66 I hope I don't have to tell you not to wear a black bra under a white blouse . . . unless you're trying to be ironic, in which case, Bravo! Here's what really matters: that you be comfortable and confident in your appearance and yourself. That should take precedence over any and all silly fashion rules or advice from well-meaning girlfriends. 99

Do you like to dress a bit sexy? A little ladylike is better in the beginning. If you're a sexy chick, it will come across. Provocative can keep his mind off your other good qualities. Don't give him any more stimulation for his southern head than he'll have from just being with a woman he's attracted to. If you want to get laid, then let it all hang out. But if that's not the message you want him to have, be subtler. Andy advises:

> ❝ Dress sexy, not trashy. Wear good shoes. And get done head to toe: hair, skin, nails, makeup. Go easy on the perfume— and wear the right perfume. Buy it for how it smells on you, not for the label. ❞

Michael McD. adds:

> ❝ I wouldn't wear anything too promiscuous. Or anything too fancy, because that can put pressure on the guy. I'd say something business casual that can go for any kind of plans. Wear something that's neutral—which doesn't send any kind of message. Not something you'd run errands in either. ❞

> "If you're a jeans and T-shirt girl who wears very little makeup, don't go out in a Cavalli dress with the entire Mac products line on your face."   —Kyle

What If His Friends Are Jerks?

Women often complain about their guys' buddies. He may be on his best behavior with you, and then become a different person— one who greatly annoys you—when he's around other guys. Should you lay down the law? Bolt? Castrate his friends? Only if his buddies are disrespectful to you. Yiannis explains:

> 66 If his friends are jerks, do nothing; if his friends are jerks TO YOU, you have to discuss it with your man. No good man is going to let anybody—especially his friends—disrespect his lady. If they treat you with respect but are just idiots in general, avoid them, but let it be. You're not going to win any points with your man by lambasting his buddies. 99

Friends who act stupid should be tolerated as much as possible. They're just being guys and having fun. Many guys don't enjoy the gossipy visits we have with our friends. Try hard not to make a big fuss. This is one of the differences between men and women that must be tolerated. You can nicely explain that you prefer the way he is when you're alone and try not to be with them too much. But don't be too negative, warns Michael T.F.:

> 66 Unless they're trying to sleep with you, don't knock his friends. You aren't married to them; he is. Consider this—without those friends around he'd be asking YOU to go fishing and to football games. Do you really need that? 99

"Don't hang with his friends if they're jerks. But they were there first."   —Andy

The friends we have the most trouble with are women. It's wrong to make him miserable because he hung out with a female friend. Don't be a jealous chick and assume that being female makes her a threat. He's with you! Be nice to her, though, since she may advise him. Don't make him lie about their interaction. Guys with female friends often make better partners. In a good relationship, each partner should respect the other's friends. Have your own friends to have fun with. Just stay alert to anyone who seems to cross over inappropriate lines.

Be Real from the Get-Go

Women put too much energy into trying to be what they think straight men want and not enough into valuing what they have. You're much better off dating a man who likes you in your real skin. If a guy you're attracted to falls for an act you put on, prepare for trouble later. Kyle sees problems if you put up a front that you can't sustain:

> 66 Honestly, the best way to go out on a first date, and yes it is cliché, is as you. If you're going out looking for a lasting relationship, then you have to avoid being misleading. Obviously, if you're going somewhere nice, dress up a little, but don't change yourself for a date. It will come back to haunt you later on. 99

Set boundaries from the start, including for YOU. In Chapter 5 we discussed this but must repeat it. Do you want to be happy with a guy? Would you prefer smiling to nagging, making love to fighting, or feeling content to being insecure? The key to creating a loving, supportive relationship with a guy is to accept him as he is from the get-go. If he's not up to your speed, don't continue.

Your choice isn't to make him a new model. You can use some of our suggestions and see how open he is to working with you. Every guy will have shticks, But make sure the overall package— his main course—is acceptable. Then see how willing he is to work with you to tweak his most annoying side dishes. Michael McD. explains:

> " Everyone has issues. Some choose to work on them. Some cop out on a relationship if the work gets to be too much. It's easier to avoid—pretend they don't exist so they don't have to confront issues. You need to look for men who are willing to do the work. These will be more emotionally available men—men who are into therapy, alternative things like meditation, and who are spiritually based. A guy must be willing to confront his shit to be ready to have a healthy relationship. Women do too. "

Jealousy Gets You Nowhere

Learn to handle his interaction with other women. Men like to look. It usually doesn't mean anything against you, so don't take it personally! You can badger a man into not looking at other women, but he'll eventually bail from the prison you create. Jealousy gets you nowhere but to Griefville. Trying to tighten the reins on him to prevent cheating will exhaust you but won't stop him. He'll eventually bail from the constraints you put on him. Dan says that when you lighten up on him, you'll have much fewer problems than if the tabs you keep are too rigid:

66 Often when you fall in love, you get very territorial. It's a natural human response but can also be damaging. People who can overcome that and don't put so much emphasis on it can actually have longer, healthier relationships. That kind of attitude makes lovers not want to stray because they feel like there's no pressure. The women I know who've gotten over that part seem to be much happier and have more fulfilling relationships. **99**

"Let men look! There's nothing wrong with looking as long as you don't touch."   —Brian

Looking at other women, or even flirting occasionally, isn't a crime. Making yourself whole on your own helps you feel secure. He has a right to go out with friends and talk to other women, as long as he doesn't pursue them. And you have a right to look at other men and enjoy the view!

"Women become obsessive and want to be with or talk to him, or know his whereabouts at ALL TIMES! That's what makes relationships sour."   —Ed

Flirting with other women in your face, all the time, is disrespectful if he knows it bothers you. If your guy constantly needs attention from other women when he's out with you, you may have to cut him loose. That's often a sign of serious insecurity. Don't play prison guard! If he's going to cheat, he'll cheat, no matter how much you stay on his case. Rick advises letting men be men as long as they just look:

66 All men look at other women. We're all built that way because we were given eyes to look. It becomes harmful when you start throwing blunt objects at your boyfriend. 99

Actually, he's more likely to cheat if you tighten the leash too much. If you trust him, give him leeway. If you don't trust him, you shouldn't stay. He should respect your feelings. Vinnie explains:

66 Whether I have a partner or not, I always like looking a lot. But it can be very insulting to the person you're with if it's often. Jealousy and anger will ultimately kill a relationship. But, I admit, I've been turned on when a partner was a little jealous. 99

Have Flexible Boundaries

Learning to accept some typical male behavior means exactly that. Accept his behavior and learn to live with it. It doesn't mean accept it today and try to change it later. Granted, guys can be exasperating. But so can we! Learning to accept his right to male behavior is easier to live with than fighting it. For example, Matthew says:

> 66 When I talk to my straight girlfriends, I tell them there is men's time and women's time. A man's sense of time and a woman's sense of time are completely different. My straight girlfriends tell me, 'I haven't heard from him in two days. He must hate my guts!' I ask them, 'What are you talking about?' Men feel they can wait a week to call you, and that's perfectly normal. That's how a buddy would call another buddy. Men aren't overeager like that. It's a difference between men's and women's cultures. Women have a need for bonding that men don't necessarily have on the same time frame. You sometimes have to work on the male, not female, schedule. My friend met a guy in Amsterdam. They e-mailed back and forth, and then he went for a week without e-mailing her and she freaked out, thinking she'd never see him again. Then he e-mailed back like nothing was wrong, because nothing was wrong. Yet in her mind it was completely over. 99

"I'm a strong believer of 'You reap what you sow.' Do I really need to elaborate on that? Ya plant corn, ya get corn."   —Ed

Get used to his ways. He'll have plenty to get used to in your behavior. Men aren't wrong when they don't do things YOUR way! Set boundaries on unacceptable stuff from the beginning.

Don't go from one extreme to another—letting him get away with too much and then trying to rein in all his behavior. Do focus on taking a stand on really unacceptable behavior. Earlier we discussed how jerks are created when we let them get away with things. If you meet a guy and become his doormat, he's going to wipe his feet on you, even if he's an otherwise nice guy. But he can't take what you don't give. Set immediately whatever tone you'd want in real life. It's not that hard to pick up on his signals if you pay attention, says Michael McD.:

66 By the first three dates you should know the person you're getting. If you listen, a man will tell you all about himself. Even if you like him, you'll know if he's unhealthy, not for you, and that you should walk away. That's probably both the strongest and hardest thing one can do. You may like someone but know he's not the right one. It's necessary to leave in the beginning, before you form attachments. Once you do, it becomes harder. 99

We often act very acquiescent with a new guy so he'll like us. Some women are nauseatingly gooey. If you like a guy, are you scared to risk that he won't like you if you show your real self? Stop sucking up at the beginning! Show the real you, right up front. Know your value. Isn't it better to be liked for the terrific woman you are and not because you're kissing up? Kyle suggests you begin in a way that shows self-respect:

66 If you want a man to treat you right, you have to show him that you have power and are self-confident from the beginning. If he sees that you're a no-bullshit kind of gal, he'll be a lot more likely

to treat you that way. If you do everything you can to please him, he'll have less respect for you, and you lose your power. 〞

> "Right off the bat you have to let them know what you expect from a relationship. Let them know in subtle ways that you won't accept secondhand treatment."   —Michael M.

Be aware of potentially unacceptable behavior so you can nip it quickly. Setting boundaries from the beginning teaches him what behavior you consider acceptable and what you don't. Force yourself to recognize the limits of what behavior you shouldn't tolerate and be prepared to walk if he crosses the line, advises Matthew:

〝 Men treat you the way you teach them to treat you. You have to draw loving boundaries. I would tell him, 'This is what my value is, and you're going to respect this value. If you're not, then maybe this isn't going to work.' Men want to hear that. 〞

If a guy really likes you and understands that treating you properly is the only way he can be with you, he can learn. If he's just there to see how much he can get from you without having to work for it or be respectful, hopefully it will be you who learns. It's your responsibility to communicate what you want and watch to see if he cares enough to make an effort. Yiannis advises taking a tough stand:

〝 The only boundary you need is 'I don't put up with any jerky behavior.' If he's a jerk from jump, move on. There are too many fish in the sea for you to waste your time trying to get a guy to treat you how you deserve. 99

If you don't stop his bad habits from the beginning, he'll continue to expect to get away with them. When you see behavior that isn't acceptable, don't wait to see if it disappears on its own. This doesn't mean being snippy or nagging him. Tell him once, nicely, why something bothers you. Then change your response (more below). Michael McD. suggests:

66 Stand your ground. Communicating correctly with men is very important. Even if you're angry, you should not come off overly angry at something he's done. Wait until you're not in an angry state to address what it is. Talk about your feelings and how it affects you, and hopefully the guy won't go on the defensive. Say what bothers you and that you don't choose to accept it. If the guy respects your feelings, he will try if he feels it's a reasonable thing not to do. Address it and talk it out. Then set a boundary for it. If the behavior continues, then he's not going to change. 99

You should also set a boundary for yourself about when it's time to leave a guy who behaves in ways that bother you. How much is enough? When he reaches the limit, enforce it if you want a healthy relationship. Vinnie explains:

66 I think we all accept dishonesty to a certain extent at the beginning of a relationship. We need to be strong enough not to

do that. From the get-go, say 'Don't bullshit me.' When we first meet someone, we want it to be perfect, so we might not be honest about who we are. That's where the problem starts, and it escalates from there. **99**

Control Him by Controlling You!

We've said this throughout the book and will give more details now. If you want more control over how your guy treats you and what you get from him, learn to control yourself and your needs. The tone you set influences your interactions with others. When you make yourself a priority, you have more control over your response to a guy you like, no matter how badly you want him.

> "You must always feel important, and let it show. YOU ARE important, not him. He has to want you, not the other way around. Don't cut yourself short."
>
> —Kevin A.

Changing your response to behavior that you don't like gives you a better shot at getting what you want. Forget fighting with him about it! That's a lose/lose situation. Nip the nagging, unless you like making him more resolute in his ways. We harp on men so much about what we don't like that they're used to ignoring us. If you respond differently, he may wonder what you're up to. That's better than directly trying to change him, David says:

> 66 The truth is that you can never change another human being. Sometimes if there are things to change, you have to be the one to change first. That, in itself, will start a series of changes. You can also change your perspective on something. Everyone is able to change, but no one can change another person. You can only change yourself. If you try to do anything but that, forget it! You're fighting a losing battle. 99

Accept that you can't change his ways directly. You can, however, send a message with your response that he might understand better than your complaints. For example, if you don't nicely accept his lame excuse when he shows up late, or you're not there at all, he may get the message. Teach him with actions instead of complaining. If he's often late, make plans with a friend instead. After getting tired of waiting for people indefinitely, Yiannis created a new policy for latecomers:

> 66 It's much easier to make changes in yourself than others. So, if you don't like waiting around on a guy, don't! I have a twenty-minute rule because I've found that twenty minutes is the amount of time I can wait for somebody—be it a friend, lover, or business associate—before I start getting pissed. So, now, I leave at nineteen minutes, saving myself the anger and my boyfriend my wrath. 99

Yelling at him for being late rarely gets him there on time for your next date. He might even come later next time as payback for your reaction. Focus on what you really want—getting him to respect your time. Punishing him won't do that. Save your energy and just make other plans.

> "Don't you deserve somebody who respects you more and does not keep you waiting? At the end of the day, he should be the one waiting for you."   —Michele

Responding sweetly to what you don't like gets much more mileage. When he pisses you off, it's tempting to tell him off. But it's more effective to turn the tables with a smile, because it works! Use diplomatic words. Since guys do hear the first time, tell him ONCE what you'd prefer, in a friendly tone. Amiably explaining gripes puts him off guard. If you're not whining, he's doesn't expect criticism. Explain once, nicely, what bothers you. Then let your actions reinforce your words. Kevin K. explains:

> 66 Rather than saying 'Don't you dare be late,' one might say 'I so much more enjoy an evening when we start on time, so we are not rushed.' How people respond to such suggestions says a world about their ability to respect one another. 99

While you won't get everything you want in a man, decide what's most important and compromise about the rest. But never forget that compromise means both of you! Carl recommends:

> 66 Any good relationship requires the art of compromise, which by definition is a type of change. The important thing is that both you and your partner are making changes as a team. It shouldn't be just you kowtowing to your boyfriend's needs and desires while he sits on the couch watching football. 99

Changing your behavior speaks louder than words. If he doesn't fix the doorknob, ask his friend to fix it. Or hire someone. He won't like either choice and might try harder next time.

If he doesn't call on time to make plans, make plans with a friend. He may not like it, but SWEETLY explain that you'd rather see him, but a friend called and he didn't. If he balks that you ask to do things with him too often, ask less frequently and make other plans. Relax and enjoy your life as you send subtle messages. But always be true to yourself! Randy emphasizes:

> 66 Don't change. Really. What you need to do is adjust. You are not looking to land a relationship with yourself (unless you're Donald Trump) or your best girlfriend (unless you feel a sudden wave of lesbianism coming on). You want a man, and although guys aren't a different species, they come awfully close. 99

Guys are used to us bugging them about what we want. If you just go on with your life, he may get the message and come around without a word. When he does, let him know how happy you are. Make him feel good. Patrick explains:

> 66 Positive reinforcement can work wonders, whereas nagging may change a few things in the short term but ultimately leads to more resentment than it's worth. Remember, straight men are no more difficult to condition than Pavlov's dogs. When your man makes a habit of shaving his back hair or sporting a more stylish haircut, reward him with primal triggers such as food, sex, or beer. 99

"Create enough space for him to walk into. If you create the space, he's either going to fill it by walking into it or he'll walk away."
—Michael A.

If he goes hot and cold, he might just be nervous about how intense it's getting between you. S-l-o-w down and ignore it. Men know that when their guard goes down, we might get too serious. So cool it and control your need to ask what's bothering him. No point. He won't tell you. Besides, he may not even know.

Just give him space. He may wonder why you don't bug him. That's good! If he thinks he may lose you, he may come around. As you know him better, you'll see what works and what doesn't. Past relationships with women affect him today. Pay attention to how he talks about them. They'll give you lots of clues about why he reacts to situations with defenses and why he may be scared of too much intimacy. David suggests:

❝ See what his mother is like. That sets a precedent for what your roles will have to be, especially if he hasn't worked out his stuff. If she was overbearing and a pain in the ass, the last thing you want to do is nag and be a pain in the ass. Be supportive and nurturing without being a wimp too. Find out what makes him tick. This is for the woman who cares about being in a relationship. Every man is different. You have to find out what he's like. ❞

The Art of Gentle Nudging

If you want your guy to be agreeable about shaping up, having his appearance upgraded, or changing some of his annoying habits, be gentle, tactful, and sweet.

> "Get him VERY TACTFULLY and with LOVE to change his bad habits! NOT in a chastising manner or in a 'You know what really irritates me about you' tone."　　　　　　　　　　**—Ed**

Ask, don't tell. Suggest, don't play Ms. Know-It-All. Your approach can determine his response. Demands and complaints push a guy's stubborn buttons. Let him think he has a say in doing what you want. Bob explains:

> 66 It's a cinch. Begin by asking his opinion, because it's not very likely he will ask yours. If it's the same as yours—go for it. If it's not, then simply proceed as you planned—and keep reminding him that you asked his opinion in the first place. He'll forget that he did not get his way. 99

Would you prefer to make a point or get your way? If it's the latter, smile, sweeten your tone, and just state or suggest what you'd like. If you say something nice first, Michael McD. says his guard may go down:

66 If a woman wants something, she should ask for it in a way that's not demanding. She could nicely say what she'd like and ask if he would mind doing it. Then the guy gets the message, it's not a game, and it doesn't come across as a demand either. Just express what you'd like. Communicate properly—don't make it a power trip or a demand. Do it as two individual adults, the same way you would communicate with a friend. 99

When you've developed a friendship with your guy, it's easier to nudge him to make some small changes. Explain what you'd like and get his input. Let him be part of the decision, as long as he does something. "What do you think, honey? How would you like me to ask you to do that in the future?" You might be surprised at his response when you stop demanding and make him feel that his thoughts and feelings count. Kevin K. advises:

66 Let him have his way, at least some of the time. But beyond that is the necessity to make a space that is not only his way or her way but also our way. 99

"When communicating with a man, simplicity is key. You must treat him as if he is a puppy, and to train a puppy you must be patient. Repetition is essential in the learning process. And we all know how rewarding it is to have a well-trained dog." —Hedda

Women complain that they don't get enough help with chores. Show him that taking care of the living space and household chores is a "we" job. Find nice ways to accomplish this. Carl says to be direct and creatively persuasive to get the job done:

> 66 If you need help around the house, you've gotta give a little to get a little. Offer to do something nice for him if he finishes mowing the lawn. Don't expect men to pick up on subtle hints. Be direct, and don't be afraid to resort to bribes and rewards of steak dinners and homemade chocolate chip cookies. 99

The biggest repair job that women undertake on their guys is to clean up his appearance. The guys are sure that you can get him to upgrade himself, if you follow their advice. The whole metrosexual thing that's been going on lately should make this a lot easier. Travis explains:

> 66 As for cleaning habits and what not, there are all sorts of products out there for men now, in really butch-looking stainless steel containers and all. If guys learn how good it feels or how good they smell (and not like flowers, mind you), I bet they will start to catch on. Also, if you respond to changes, like better clothes or new haircuts, they will get the drift. Worst-case scenario: Take him out shopping with a gay friend who can show him up. Maybe his competitive nature will start to come out. 99

"Don't ASSUME responsibility for chores in the first place just because you're a woman."   —Ed

If your rooster should be hiding instead of strutting his head, Fritz suggests that you get him a gift certificate to your hairdresser. Compliment him (during sex, if possible) if he looks good when he gets a good haircut. Remember Pavlov's dogs. Don't insult what you don't like. Reward him for the good. Michael McD. adds:

" Don't put him down or compare him to other people. Don't buy him stuff. That can backfire. I would try to compliment him when he does dress up. Say it's a turn-on. Try to boost his self-esteem to want to dress up more rather than knocking him down for not doing it. "

Help him come up with your idea. When he sees how nice it is to upgrade his grooming, he may allow you to help him think of things he should do. It's great if you can be straight with him, but that's often hard. Yiannis recommends using positive actions instead of words to gently nudge him:

" If you're not comfortable talking it over with your man—and that's a whole different problem—I say go with positive reinforcement. Show (don't tell) him how much the scent of him turns you on, right as he's coming out of the shower. Initiate some kisses if he shows up clean shaven. Let him know what it does to you to see him in a suit or with his nails neatly manicured. Focus on the positive—

how much you like it when he (fill in the blank), not the negative—
how much you hate it when he (fill in the blank). If that doesn't
work, bribe him. Promise to wear his favorite dress if he'll put on
a tie."

"I had a woman come who made her husband try on jeans that
she loved and he hated. She made him wear them. Do you really
want to mold him into something like a doll? He is what he is.
Don't go too far."   —Glenn

Practice what you preach. Make sure that you groom yourself
well and allow him to enjoy it before broaching his grooming.
Often in a relationship, we let ourselves go too. If you look nice, it's
a better motivation for him. Hedda agrees:

66 You should deal with him directly in a straightforward manner. But I do believe you should deal with him while looking your
best. Put on your favorite outfit, and style your hair the way he likes
it. This way he'll be so overwhelmed by the way you look that he
will say 'yes' to anything. 99

Men don't have the same version of clean as we do. We like
squeaky clean. Many guys believe clean is when they are not dirty
or think that changing the sheets should happen when they smell.
Slowly get him used to your version of clean.

"As for that fetid heterosexual funk emanating from your betrothed, try enticing him into hygiene by suggesting a hot and steamy shower together." —Patrick

Be a little more tolerant if you want to reach common ground. Many of us don't understand how he can wear underwear with overt stains or not be concerned if he spends the weekend with you unexpectedly and has no clean clothes with him. But many men don't worry about stuff like that. Show him with appreciation why he'll enjoy the benefits of good grooming. Keoni suggests emphasizing the positive benefits of alterations:

66 Explain any change you want you to implement as a value in presenting himself to the world in the best light. Reframe what isn't working to being the best he can be. Share with him why some men care and how attending to details gets them more. Every man wants more. Sports and other industries now have men as well tailored as a gay man and completely straight. If that doesn't work, settle down for an evening of Bravo and let the Fab 5 get your man up to par. 99

Grooming together can make it more pleasant for him. Kind, gentle, and loving gestures can turn your slob into a hottie. A guy can be gently nudged to upgrade his appearance and habits if you make him feel good about doing so. Try David's recommendations:

❝ If he's a slob, make sure he has a good haircut. When he comes out of the shower say, 'Honey, let me comb your hair for you.' Be loving and gentle when you clean him up a little bit, and he might begin to feel it isn't so bad. He might like the way you're treating him if you're being sweet. Give him a kiss and comb his hair and put some cologne on him and moisturizer on his face while saying 'I love you. I just want you to look good tonight, and I'm going to help you a little.' Let him see it's not bad to let you help him. It's all in your approach. What man wouldn't want his woman taking care of him? Say something like 'I've picked some clothes out for you. Do you like them? Are you comfortable with that shirt? No? Then let's try something else. This event is really important to me, so I'd like you to look really nice. Let's figure out what you can put on.' It can be a mutual effort. A straight man is not a fashion maven. And if he is a fashion maven, that's a whole other issue. Then, honey, you need to talk to me. There's something he may be telling you that he doesn't know yet. **❞**

First-Aid Tips

- Plan a vacation or activity that you can look forward to in the future.
- Write down everything you want in a man. Then check off the ones that are imperative to have, like fun to be with, trustworthy, intelligent, responsible. Keep it handy.
- Repeat "I deserve a man who makes me happy."

9

REVOLVE AROUND YOURSELF!

Developing a Life That Attracts Healthy Men

"Follow your dreams and no one else's.
Live each day to the fullest."

—Kevin A.

We've discussed the importance of completing yourself. My motto is "If you want a man, get a life." There's nothing more powerful in a relationship than having a full life that revolves much more around you than around him. Having a life that's good, with or without a man, minimizes the fear you can get about losing a guy you're seeing. Fear keeps you stuck with unacceptable guys—way too long, especially if you think life is incomplete without one. A man may be initially flattered if you make him your world, but it gets old fast. It can lead to being taken for granted or even abuse. And revolving around him sure won't motivate his best behavior! A happy, independent woman is hotter!

Men are more attracted to happy women who don't have signs of "needy" on their faces. They like a challenge. There's nothing like the intrigue of a woman with a life to make a man work to find a place in it, adds Kevin S.:

> **“** Men like a woman who believes in herself, seems to be happy, has some direction, and draws the line when he goes too far. Men feel a strong woman has a clue about what life is supposed to be about. **”**

There's been a lot of hype about figuring out whether a guy is, or is not, that into you. Why not create a happy life that makes a guy wonder if you're that into him?! When you have a life of your own, you're busy enjoying it. That gives you less time to worry about whether he's into you or not. You'll find out if he makes the effort to please you. If not, you can continue living without him instead of trying to find ways to lure him back. If he is into you, his effort will be more pronounced when he sees you're not in need of him to be happy. So, if you want a man, get a life! Use this chapter to begin to develop one that's satisfying, without a man being the center of it.

Why Your Life Is More Important Than HIM

Do you settle for guys who hurt you or deplete your happiness? Are his sweet crumbs worth it? Be honest! If you're not strong enough to leave, don't, at least not yet. But perk up your awareness of how he treats you as you get stronger by building your self-esteem, and your life. Stay, but work on you. Eventually you'll be strong enough to drop the excuses and leave, because you have a life without him too. Kyle explains:

" When you've created a healthy life of your own, if the time comes for you to get out of the relationship, you will be able to discern that it's time to leave and realize that it is for the best. Always remember that you don't need a man to survive, not even the most amazing man you've ever met. You are always enough on your own. Search for things you can do on your own that make you feel happy and fulfilled. When you are around people, make sure they are supportive of you and your endeavors. Once your time is being occupied by things that you enjoy doing and the people whom you spend time with are positive influences, independence will come to you and you'll love it! "

When you leave a guy who isn't good for you, you can either mourn—which keeps the pain alive—or you can rejoice—which empowers you. Embrace the fact that you were strong enough to leave, that you're rid of him, and that you can create a happier life without him. The guys and I have suggestions for how to take control of your happiness by developing a life that doesn't depend on anyone. Vinnie explains:

" If you're clear about who you are, what your goals are, how you want to be treated, and you're solid in that place—you don't need to act a certain way. You won't need a plan. Either you're treated the way you want to be treated or you leave. Being secure in the fact that you are complete just as you are is so attractive and sexy. You won't have to go on a manhunt. Men will be knocking down the door. There's nothing sexier than a person who is comfortable in his or her own skin. "

When your life revolves around a guy, you may delude yourself that you're complete when you're with someone. The trouble is— if you're nothing without him, you're actually nothing when you're with him too. Being his life isn't your life! Keoni says that independence is also the ability to work on your interdependence with the strengths of others:

> 66 We can each add more when we can truly take good care of ourselves and continue to play nicely with others. The best place to start being independent is by seeking to first understand a need or problem for oneself and then to create a plan to resolve the problem or fulfill the need. When a woman is independent and confident, she can interact interdependently with a man or independently when the circumstances dictate. 99

When your happiness doesn't depend on a guy, you don't have to stay with one who's just okay or who you see as better than nothing. Why waste time with men who aren't into you enough to treat you well? Appreciate having more time for friends and things you love. A great life gives you power with men because they don't feel sure of you the way they are with women who revolve around them.

> "You cannot be in a healthy relationship with anyone else if you aren't in one with yourself. To have autonomy and be able to be with yourself is a huge gift. It's throwing something away if you can't do it."   —Rick

Learn to Enjoy Being Solo

The best way to attract a healthy relationship is to do concrete things to become a healthier person. That takes time, but it's better than going from one unhappy relationship to another. Be loving to yourself by spending extra on things you enjoy. Indulge yourself when you can—a massage, good lotion, flowers, a good restaurant, etc.

Often we're more practical about treating ourselves than spending on others, especially a guy we like. Be realistic. If your bills are paid, enjoy a little splurging. Do things you enjoy on your own, happily. Take pleasure in being able to do what you want, when you want it, and on your own terms. My first meal solo felt weird, until I realized how nice it was to read in a restaurant with no interruptions. Ed recommends:

    " A woman should develop independence to live a mentally sane, healthy existence. If she has that, then everything else in life is like icing on the cake (men, money, etc.). To go about it, I would suggest seeking out books about finding your TRUE identity, 'the real you.' If that's not your bag, try spending time ALONE sitting in a quiet place with your eyes closed for about ten minutes a day. Let your mind free itself of any stressful thoughts, and relax. Over time, you'll learn a LOT about yourself. **"**

If you have a boyfriend you sort of know isn't right for you or who lets you down a lot, it's empowering to know you have options. Enjoy his goodies, but be honest about what bothers you.

Don't shut your mouth with him and stew to friends. Speak up. If he pushes you too far, leave with no regrets.

Don't you get tired of trying to find a friend to join you when you want to do something? Try an activity on your own, and pay attention to the benefits of doing it all your way. It might take time to get used to it. But one day you may realize that you prefer your own company once you spend some time alone. No dating. Get to know yourself. Learn the joy of eating out alone and being able to have what you—not he—are in the mood for. Doing things YOUR way can be lots of fun. Solitude can teach that there's a great life beyond a man. A complete woman is a happy one! Travis explains that everyone needs to be happy with themselves before they can happily date:

    " No way does anyone need someone, be it a man or a woman, to complete themselves. A friend of mine in the navy once said to me that if you are comfortable enough to go to a movie by yourself, you are comfortable enough with yourself to date someone. I thought it was odd until I realized I had never actually gone to a movie theater and seen a movie by myself. When you are comfortable with yourself, it shows, and that makes you a lot more attractive. **"**

Thinking about seeing a movie solo used to seem intimidating and unappealing. Now I enjoy just going when I feel like it, often at the last minute. I've learned to appreciate how nice it is to go places on my own and to plan solo trips in advance that I can look forward to. I'm happy to go with someone I enjoy being with, but it's nice knowing I'm not dependent on having someone go with me. That led to unhealthy choices in the past.

It's nice to decide to go somewhere at the last minute and not waste time calling around to find someone to go with. Doing activities on your own develops autonomy. Autonomy helps you develop confidence, which is very attractive. Michael M. advises:

66 If you're just an empty vessel out looking for a husband all the time, you're not appealing. There are a lot of people who want to get married, but plenty of them have more to offer. Don't panic if you have a night or weekend alone. Realize that you're a grownup and that you should have cultivated enough inner resources that you can be your own best friend and be good company for yourself. You don't need to be with somebody all the time. 99

"Get rid of everything that your mother told you in the past. I don't think it works any longer. Everything has changed so much."

—Jason

We put tons of energy into reading books to understand and please men but spend little time understanding what makes us happy beyond a man and recognizing our strengths. Go for a meal with a book or magazine. Get one ticket for a show or concert. Dress nicely and take yourself out. It's more relaxing when you don't have to worry about anyone else. More single women do things solo. Join them! Consider how your life would be if it didn't include a man, says Matthew:

66 Think about 'What if I didn't need a man? What would I do with my life?' Take the man out of the picture, like it's a science fiction movie, and come from that place. Pretend that you don't need a man for anything, period. Then imagine what you would do with your life, time, motivation, and energy. Men, people, in general, are extra. If you rely on anybody, you come from a place of weakness. Yeah, people do need people. But if you feel completely incomplete as a soul without a man, that's not right. 99

As your self-esteem grows, you'll feel more comfortable doing things solo. And the more nice things you do solo, the greater your self-esteem will get. It's a lovely cycle that you'll enjoy once you get over your initial discomfort. Kevin S. advises:

66 Find out what interests you. What are you about? What do you like to do? Stop trying to be what everyone else wants you to be and figure out who you are, what makes you happy, and what makes you tick. 99

"You need to be secure in yourself. Find enjoyment and comfort in your own company. Nail this, and you'll be more attractive to a man."
—Andy

When you feel strong and beautiful on the inside, it radiates out. Enjoying your own company rocks! So does the company of great friends, without the guys along. Cultivate friendships with people you enjoy spending time with. Even if you're in a relationship, plan a FUN weekend getaway with just the girls—somewhere you can just have a blast and leave your worries at home. You'll still want to be with your guy, but it's nice to have choices. Going out and doing your own things gives you something to share when you're with your partner. Find a good balance. Alex empathizes that since we all need connections to special people, it's hard to do without. But waiting until you have your own life before you get into a relationship is worth it:

66 It's incredibly difficult to tell yourself that you don't need anyone, because you do. We're social creatures and need to be around people and find meaningful relationships. You have to be patient and make yourself a better partner. When you become a complete person, you don't want someone who is a half. You want somebody who's also complete. Do anything you can do to take care of yourself physically and spiritually. It makes you a better, more attractive woman. 99

Do you still wonder how to get a life? Pursue activities that interest you. Give yourself things to look forward to, either with a friend or solo. Plan a vacation, even if it takes a year to save for it. Make arrangements to see friends you can't see often. Get tickets to something you'd enjoy. Life feels better when goodies are on the horizon. Do volunteer work. It's satisfying to help others; it enables you to meet potential friends, and it can teach valuable skills. Do these things even when you're in a relationship! Yiannis explains why solo time is important even when you have a partner:

" It's very easy to get lost in a relationship. If you find yourself relying on your man for too much, do something alone that's all about you. Learn a language, take a dance class, prepare for a marathon, etc. The activity itself doesn't matter nearly as much as the feeling of independence you'll gain by having something that's all your own. "

Make Choices Based on Your Own Needs

Women are known for not being able to make up their minds. Think about what you'd like to have or do or say. If your decisions are based on what you think others want you to choose, you're not being true to you!

Do you agree to things that would make Mom happy? Have you done things that friends say you "should"? When your guy asks where you'd like to eat or what you'd like to do, are you conflicted by what he'd like you to choose or your own true preference? I used to answer those kinds of questions with another question—"What would you like?" Then I'd waffle with making a choice because I didn't know whether to choose what would please HIM or me. A confident woman weighs her choices and picks the best one for her. People ask what you want because they want to know. You can do that if you choose to. Practice making your choices personal, one at a time! Glenn insists:

" Women are known for not making up their minds. What do you want? If someone tells you something and you want it but then someone tells you that you don't, and you can't make a decision, you're not making up your own mind. Make up your mind on your own! 🙴

Once you identify your true desires, it's easy to know what to choose. Base your decisions on YOU, not HIM. Get in touch with why you think you need a guy so much. If necessary, go for therapy. Meanwhile, keep developing your life. It will increase your power and help to maintain it in a relationship. Make a satisfying life more important than a manhunt! You don't need a guy to fix things or protect you! Take classes and learn how to do things yourself. You can become self-sufficient without a man, but you don't have to be Supergirl. There are people you can hire to do the things you can't do or don't want to, says Jason:

🙴 You don't need to learn to do everything—just get a handyman or a good housekeeper. You can buy all this stuff. I grew up with all this. It's about having a great list of people to call for help. 🙴

"Educate yourself really fiercely. Make sure you do what you want with your life. Make your own money, and make sure you can stand on your own two feet." —Kevin A.

Educate yourself about money matters. Don't be afraid of them. You may not like money stuff. But create good spending habits and create a plan to always put something away. Women need to create financial power. A fantastic resource is Jean Chatzky's book *Make Money, Not Excuses: Wake Up, Take Charge, and Overcome Your Financial Fears Forever*. If you don't know how, learn to balance a checkbook. When you save some money, find out your options for investing or buying something with equity like an apartment, instead of just leaving it in the bank for security. We often let our guy handle money decisions. Financial independence is another way to lessen your reliance on men. And he'll know you're there for him, not security. Take charge of your money, even if you're in a relationship, so you never feel stuck, advises Carl:

> ❝ Keep that pocketbook to yourself! Even if you have a joint account with your partner, always have an account on the side that only you can access. Squirrel away a little money out of every paycheck—even if it's only ten dollars a week. It'll add up, and you'll always have a safety cushion should anything go wrong. And if your relationship remains strong, as we all hope it will, you'll eventually have a big piggy bank to use as a down payment on a house, car, or whatever you need. ❞

Let him compete with your life, instead of being IT. If he knows you have many interests when he's not around, he'll have to work harder. Let him see why you won't stick around if he doesn't make you happy—you have better things to do!

> "Carrie Bradshaw got Big when she lost interest. Make your guy compete for your attention by making other things as important as he is."
> —Kyle

Keep Your Friends!

Do you forget your friends when you're in a relationship? Many women do. Besides being unfair to them, it's not good to let your man be more important than friends. It's all too common among women—when someone gets into a relationship they kind of drop off their friends' social radar. Do you only spend time with friends when you're between relationships?

If you're involved in a relationship, it's normal to spend a lot of time with your guy. But don't cut off friends! Many women don't value the essence of friendship—the best support system—and don't see girlfriends as the gold they are. Instead, we turn to them when there's no one else. But your friends aren't stupid. Eventually you won't be valued either, which hurts when you need them. Kevin S. explains:

66 Don't dump your girlfriends or a previous date with them to go out with a man, period. It shows disability—that you're nothing when you don't have a man. It also tells the women around you that they're nothing really in your life except a spongy support group. 99

"Whether your friends are male or female, they are so important. At the end of the day, if anything happens to your relationship, your friends are there. They're there before the relationship and after the relationship."   —Kevin A.

Make plans to see friends when you can and keep in touch by phone. If you break up, you'll get support. If you only call friends when the guy is gone, prepare to mourn on your own. Rick emphasizes the importance of maintaining the friendships that have sustained you in the past—because they will most likely be the ones remaining with you in the future:

> 66 Men come and go. Your friends are there always. Giving up everything for a man is such a bad thing to do. If you give up on your friends, when he dumps you—and he will if you've made him the center of your universe—then what do you have? Your friends are gone, and he's gone. You'd better be really happy with yourself because that's all you have. But if you've made a man the center of everything in the first place, that indicates that you're not happy with yourself. 99

It's wrong to cancel plans at the last minute because HE calls. Don't do that to friends! If something really special comes up, be honest with a girlfriend and ask if she'd mind if you postponed plans this one time. But don't make it a habit. Michael M. explains:

> 66 It's awful to be canceled because there's suddenly a boyfriend who you know isn't going to last anyway. Friendship lasts longer than most relationships. Don't screw with your friends' schedules. Your friends are there for you through thick and thin. When you're in a relationship and when you're not, they deserve to be treated like gold. 99

"Don't ever ditch your friends or whine to them. Whining should be to your shrink."   —Vinnie

If your life includes friends, give them equal treatment. Laugh with them! Have fun. Show the appreciation for them that they deserve. And if your friends aren't fun to be with, make new ones. But friends should have a special place of honor in the life you create. And a guy who you're seeing should be seen as a visitor, until he's earned more over a long period of time.

Redefining Solo

Are you afraid of being lonely without a guy? What is lonely? It does not mean being alone! Spending time alone can be rewarding. Feeling a loss of connection and love from people, and yourself, creates loneliness. Dan further explains:

66 A lot of people don't want to go out alone or be seen as a lonely person because they confuse *lonely* with *loner*. They can be happy on their own but are pressured to feel like they should be with somebody and don't want to go to the movies alone. I find that preposterous! 99

"You can feel lonely in a crowd."   —Kevin S.

When you're confident in yourself, you can enjoy alone time. Lonely is a state that can make you depressed, even with others around. Lonely is an emotion—feeling a void that you must try to fill. But others can't do that for you past the moment. Only YOU can be the antidote to loneliness. When you're in a relationship, be happy when your guy has things to do instead of anticipating loneliness when he's out. More time for you! Alex says that time spent apart enhances a relationship:

66 I've been in a relationship where my boyfriend liked to be alone a lot. Women can learn a lot by letting their partners have their alone time. Otherwise they can suffocate their partners. They need to learn to be alone. That shouldn't be a problem for someone who is complete. 99

A lot of women hurt themselves in the name of loneliness. "I let him get away with abusive talk because I couldn't stand being lonely if he left." We make poor choices to avoid being alone. Don't stay with a guy who doesn't treat you well or just settle for someone. Too many women feel lonely when they're in relationships. You must fill your own voids. Being alone can be lovely when you take the bad onus off it. Rick explains:

66 I love being alone. Being lonely is completely different. You feel you need someone to complete you, or your insecurities are such that you aren't validated unless you have someone else to do it for you. You have to be able to validate yourself. I love to be alone with a book and a bath. I run a bath, light some candles, get some nice slippery lotion, and validate myself at least twice a week. 99

I also do the bath, with candles, soft music, bubbles, and some wine or tea, as often as I can. ME time! As we said earlier, try doing things you enjoy solo. Have good music playing at home. Make your home a cheerful place to be and enjoy the vibe. Make an effort to make your bed and keep your place neat. That's a visible reminder of taking control. And keep showing yourself love. One of the greatest joys is to realize how much you look forward to solo time. You're not alone. You're spending time with you. That's a joy, not a sentence. Remember—alone does not mean lonely! You don't have to be scared of time without anyone. It makes you a healthier person and more attractive to men. Ed explains:

    ❝ People are healthier when they have time alone to spend with themselves. Hell, if YOU can't spend time alone with yourself and be content, what makes you think ANYONE ELSE wants to spend time alone with you? ❞

"Being alone is a state of being, while being lonely is emotional—a state of mind." —Alex

Nurture Your Spiritual Side

Having a spiritual mind-set helps you to be stronger on the inside. Faith creates the inner power that enables you to have more control over how you let men treat you. Many of the guys encourage you to find whatever concept of faith works for you. You have to find your own comfortable path to creating inner peace and balance, a belief in a higher power or an anchor for your faith.

Whether it's tied to religion, nature, or something very different, the most important thing is to use it! Rick defines the effects of spirituality like this:

> 66 Any type of spiritual practice puts you in touch with who you really are, your real true value as a human being and what you have to contribute. It gets you in touch with a real appreciation of your life at every single moment. No matter what the circumstance, it can't help but propel you forward in your life and your relationships with people. It also gives you the confidence not to grab the crumbs but to go for the whole loaf. 99

Developing spiritual confidence can keep fear in check. It's comforting to trust that you'll get what you need. Spiritual faith is a big power tool. If you already have some faith, nurture it by using it more. If you trust that everything will work out okay, it usually does. It might not be exactly what you hoped for or would have liked, but it does work out, if you let it. Kevin A. believes a spiritual sense of self directly relates to relationships:

> 66 I think a spiritual foundation is good for you. If you put it out that you're only open to men with specific qualities, you limit yourself. Trust that the right man will enter your life, without restriction. Then go on with your life if you really believe it. 99

"We all need to believe in ourselves completely before we can even begin to believe in others."   —Randall

Allow spiritual power to nurture more faith in you. If you know that when the time is right a good man will be there, you can relax and enjoy life now, as I do. You may need to make yourself healthier before meeting him. Meanwhile, your life can keep improving so there will be more to share when it's time.

All you need is ONE good man, and those who aren't right for you don't matter. Stay focused on making yourself happier, and allow faith to help you wait for a man who makes you happy. Michael A. says that we need infinite patience to find the right guy and infinite patience to live with the right guy:

66 Faith gives you more patience, which is great practice for when you get the guy. Then you'll need all the patience you can get! 99

"You have to have faith in the world and how it works and in your-self for those times when you want a man but don't have one."

—Michael M.

No matter what level your belief system is at, at least make an effort to test your spiritual power so you can relax more and trust that life works out if you let it. When you're frustrated about not having a man in your life, count your blessings. Write down every little thing you like in your life—the people, hobbies, your apartment, sunshine, good health, and so on. Focus on the good you have instead of what's missing. Be happy with what's in your life. When you worry less, you get more. Creating a happy life does that, and faith sustains it.

First-Aid Tips

- Make a play date with yourself. Do things that you enjoy, YOUR way. Plan an entire day, or weekend, doing things you enjoy on your own.
- List things that you have been afraid to try or that you don't think you can do yourself, like checking your vehicle's oil or learning new computer skills. Find a class or someone who can teach one to you.
- List things you enjoy that contribute to your happiness, and don't involve a man, and find ways to do them even when you're in a relationship.
- Get more batteries for your vibrator!

10

WANTED—ONE SPERM DONOR, MUST BE FINANCIALLY SECURE

How to Put Marriage and Children into Perspective

"I look at relationships like plants. You can't sit and force a tree or yell at it to grow faster."
—*Matthew*

He's having fun. You're having fun. Time to spoil it! You and your friends think it's time to move forward. You bring it up. He hedges. You get angry. He gets defensive. You try to discuss. He becomes mute. You accuse him of not caring. He gets furious that you don't know how much he cares. You stop having fun. He stops having fun. You read him his rights—the ones you and your girl-friends create. He balks, saying he's not ready. But you push until he gets fed up and leaves. Then you and your friends discuss why many men don't want to commit. Matthew says:

66 There's such an emphasis on traditional values—getting married and having kids—and it's fine and dandy. There's nothing wrong with that. But what's lost sometimes are deeper issues—Are you secure as a human being, first and foremost? Who are you?

And do you accept that it's okay to be single? Women have a lot of issues, like the biological clock or peer pressure because their girlfriends are getting married. That can make a woman eager and rush her into something. You are strong and complete as a woman. My own mother taught me that. I think gay men understand that a little better because they have a different relationship with their mothers than straight men do. I always respected a woman's power. Yet many women today don't. **"**

New Agenda: Have Fun!

Men don't have to live by our agendas! There's no law mandating how fast a guy must commit or that he must get married at all. Women aren't the almighty dictators of relationship rules and agendas. It is often too soon to know if a guy is the right person to marry or have kids with. Yet, as Kevin K. sees it, women accept what friends say as a directive and do everything to make it happen:

" Heterosexual women and men are often foisted into prescribed roles of spouse and parent from socialization and roles that are taught to take care of sexual and intimacy needs. The problem is that this happens before they have the opportunity to really know themselves, their individual needs and wants, including the specifics of their sexual pleasure. When a woman really knows those desires, which develop and change with maturity, she brings to a relationship desires that can be satisfied. Otherwise there is an indefinable longing that leaves the partner guessing and her dissatisfied. Knowing these wants, needs, and desires is a strong foundation. 〝〝

Cool your agendas for a while. Men do want relationships. But they're scared pups who need to ease into a serious relationship slowly and will pull back no matter what they desire if there's too much pressure. Focus on having fun instead of immediately analyzing his husband potential. Rick advises:

❝ Go on a date without an agenda and experience it for what it is with no expectations. That's the beginning. Approach it like a man—as a fun time. It may not have a future after midnight. Think of your date as a complete relationship in one evening. There is a beginning, a middle, and an end in one night, period. Then you'll have a good time. 〝〝

What's More Important: His Wallet or His Love?

"A woman who chases men with money is bound to wind up emotionally bankrupt in the end."　　　　**—Kyle**

Men still complain they need resumes to date some women. How cold we can get! One of the biggest gripes men have is what they call "mercenary women." Everybody wants to be loved for themselves, not how much they can buy for you.

"Look at him as an individual, not as an insurance policy."

—Fritz

Guys don't like being wanted as a security blanket. Maybe less attractive ones do since they know money can still buy them a decent-looking woman if they show enough credit-card love. Michael M. suggests:

    “ You can make money yourself. It's not a level playing field in the working world yet, but women have more opportunities than in the past. A more admiral ambition is 'I'm going to make money and be successful' than to hook up with someone for money. If you hook up with a rich guy just for money, it sets the whole relationship off balance. He becomes in charge of all the decisions—he's the boss and using you for something because you're using him for something. True love goes right out the window. **”**

Some men have become so sensitive that they bristle with suspicion when a woman even asks what he does for a living. A materialist approach makes a relationship harder to work, says Yiannis:

    “ If you measure the success of a date by how much money a man is spending on you, you're establishing a pattern of him showing you with money how he feels for you. That's fine, if it's what you want, but I'd rather have a man who shows me how he feels with backrubs, by listening to what I say, and by giving me his jacket when I'm cold. **”**

A man with money impresses our friends and family, especially Mom, so she can brag to her friends about her daughter's financially secure guy. The media presents expensive gifts of jewelry and being taken out in style as a show of love. Your mom and your girlfriends reinforce it. But it's not. Far from it! Men with limited funds are just as capable of loving you. Love comes from actions and the way he treats you, not his bank account. Michael McD. warns:

> Looking for money is an unreal situation. You'll have an unhappy existence. Whenever you look for materialistic things, you're not really interested in the person. You're interested in what he has to offer. For you to truly love someone and experience true intimacy, you have to see the person for who they are, not for what they can give you. That attitude is a self-fulfillment thing of needing to fill a void and get taken care of.

Would you rather have a guy who shows his love by spending money on you or one who makes you feel special with the way he treats you? The latter will keep you warm and fuzzy at night. It's fine to want a man who can take care of himself. But couples fall in love, not into better solvency. Kevin K. sees an unpleasant reality of being involved with a wealthy man:

> I have observed that men with lots of money are often looking for the 'trophy wives' and have little to offer in return, often not even their money because they keep such a tight rein on it. There is nothing wrong with this game as long as you are aware of the field on which you play.

You limit opportunities with great men when you put a price tag on a guy and might miss a great one because you don't think he earns enough. But he might one day. Some men say that they're on their guard and don't divulge their income. There's so much more to a guy than his bank account! Randall has seen how having lots of money doesn't necessarily make a person happy:

> 66 I once worked for an extremely rich woman on the Upper East Side. She was so miserably unhappy, she never left her bedroom. Sure, the sheets she slept on had the highest possible thread counts, but all the money in the world wasn't enough to get her to climb out of her bed. Money is important to live, but it is no substitute for actually living a real life. 99

> "There's nothing worse than entering into a relationship with a man who thinks he owns you, because—for all practical purposes—you've given your consent to this notion."   —Patrick

You don't need a fortune to have a good life with a terrific guy. Money doesn't buy love, even if you love his money. A guy who loves what he does, without a huge salary, will make you happier than one who's obsessed with making tons of money in a stressful job he hates. A happy guy is more likely to spread the joy. Patrick sees it this way:

> 66 Money is not a bad place to start, but make certain the rest of the chips fall into place. There's nothing wrong with seeking a

man with professional prowess and a platinum Visa card. Many times that success may carry over into his personal life, while other men may have sacrificed so much to their careers that their interpersonal relationship skills are nil. **"**

Don't Make Marriage More Important Than the Guy

Are you so obsessed with getting married that the wedding and being a bride are your top priorities? Being on a mission to get married mucks up most everything else, making it difficult to create a satisfying life. Carl advises you to keep the importance of marriage in a realistic perspective:

" Having marriage or a life partner as a goal is certainly admirable (though not required, no matter what society tells you). The problem is when marriage becomes your ONLY goal that overrides all others. I just don't see how this can be healthy, because if the marriage thing doesn't work out for some reason, then you're left with a big hole in your heart and your head. Far better I think is to have several major life goals, which might include marriage, children, a rewarding career, life-affirming friendships, community work, church, etc. **"**

"Women who marry because they feel they HAVE TO are usually the same women who end up getting a divorce because they HAVE TO to protect their sanity."   —Randall

Marrying a guy for any reason other than love limits happiness. Committing to a guy who doesn't stimulate your passion gets tedious. And screaming kids with a man you don't have a close intimate bond with can sink the dream of marriage and family fast. If you wake up one morning and don't feel a warm glow when you look at the guy you married to get married, or you can't bear the thought of watching him grow old, or having sex with him evokes a strong need for batteries and fantasies—it may be too late to ask yourself if the marriage and kids were worth it. Michael M. points out why it's best not to rush to say "I do":

❝ There were days when you had to be married by twenty-one, but they're over. If it's not meant to happen at that moment, don't force it. Otherwise you'll be stuck in some hideous marriage. Most marriages end in divorce. You don't want to be just another statistic. Relax and have a little faith in yourself. **❞**

Create your own security and enjoy life much more! If you slowly expand yourself as a woman, exploring different men and developing your sense of self as you go, you have the best shot at attracting a guy who'll rock your world and make you feel secure for the right reasons. Making marriage your vocation gets in the way of life's pleasures. Unhappy relationships usually result when you make marriage more important than finding a special friend and lover. Men smell the urgency it creates and run. It comes across as desperation, even if you see it as just going after what you want. If you finally hook the guy, the rest of the process can be wrapped around you, and he becomes an accessory for the fantasy lifestyle you went after, according to Matthew:

> 66 You need to understand that while men have ego trips, women do too. In the same way that men have their porn, you have emotional porn. When I see bridal magazines and bridal television shows, I look at them and think, it's all about YOU—YOU and your wedding dress and who YOU can invite. And your bridesmaids. The groom is like an afterthought, just this thing. The more I see this, the more I realize in the same way that men objectify women's bodies, women do that to men all the time. You are the problem too. Women complain how in action movies there's a girlfriend who doesn't mean anything and is just window dressing. If you watch chick flicks, I'm sorry but it's the same thing. They have some poorly drawn guy character who is just there as this guy to marry. It goes both ways. You need to be more real about yourself and the peer pressure you get. 99

> "Women who are on a mission to get married are like third-party candidates trying to run for president. Both are exercises in futility, and no matter what they say, the candidates come off looking pathetic."   —Michael T.F.

Many of the guys said that a woman consumed with getting married has a problem she needs to deal with. Be careful about setting a marriage goal that rules your life. When you relax more and develop your life, many more men may come your way. Michele warns that the sheer desperation to get to the altar is counterproductive:

> 66 I do believe in the importance and the value of the family. However, being on a mission to get married sounds to me like being desperate, so I would have pity for these women. From the hairdresser's point of view, very often they can be the most difficult clients—extremely insecure, and never happy, as if the hairstyle should do it all. 99

Only YOU can make you happy. Find that happiness first. Get therapy if this is a big shtick for your life. Develop the kind of life we talked about in the previous chapter that includes, but doesn't dwell on, being with a healthy partner. Meanwhile, relax and have fun. Happiness on your own is the strongest foundation for finding happiness with someone else.

The Clock That Keeps on Ticking

Is your biological clock ticking out of control? Be careful! That clock can bring desperation to the next level. It's natural for women to want kids, so don't let others self-righteously tell you to get off your biological clock and move on. Men have no right to judge a woman who wants to be a mom. And it hurts when they do. But many women see children as their key to happiness. Kids can add to a happy life you've already created, but they won't give you one, says Patrick:

" Do not bring children into the equation as a fix-all for a bad relationship or marriage. Nothing breeds contempt like a pricey obligation that requires a constant change of diapers—especially if the male in question is not mentally, financially, or emotionally prepared for it. If something is wrong in your relationship, work on fixing it before considering children. Bringing a child into a relationship may be good for a few months of feigned marital reinvigoration, but it won't fix the underlying problem. Fix problems with counseling, not procreation."

"Figure out what's important: family or the idea of a family? That's where the work is. Figure out what you really want, not just what you think you should want."   —Vinnie

Some women believe they're supposed to get married and have a baby. The program is so strong that it's hard to be objective about whether they truly want it or want to do what's expected of them. Some women think a baby will provide the unconditional love they never got from anyone. Some hope it will make their guy stay. And some women are so unhappy they look to a baby to change that. A baby will not fix your life! Carl asks:

" First of all: Who's setting this clock? Is it your nagging mom and Aunt Vera? Is it your college girlfriends who've all had three kids apiece while you're still a single working girl? The pressure that society puts on women to have children isn't fair, especially when you consider that having kids isn't the best thing for all women —maybe most women or some women, but not ALL women. If you really do want a child and you're still single, remember that there are options. While having two parents in the household certainly makes the job easier, it's not required, no matter what the pope says. **99**

Too many women do whatever they can to find a guy to have a baby with. Many regret it when reality hits. Kids don't thrive when the parents have problems with each other. And trust me, babies aren't all fun. After the glow of new motherhood wears off and a screaming toddler stresses you up the wazoo, you'll have to turn to the sperm donor for comfort. If you don't have a loving relationship with him, it can be unhealthy for the kids. Like a man, a baby won't make you happy, if you're not happy on your own. Kyle advises:

66 If you get into a relationship simply because you want someone to father a child, you are being misleading to the man and putting yourself into a situation where you could very possibly become unhappy with your decision. This man could potentially be present in the rest of your life. If you find out later that he's someone who you don't like or want around, it may be too late. **99**

Don't rush into motherhood unless it's for healthy reasons and you can raise the child in a nurturing environment. If you're not sure, wait. Ask yourself if you want a baby because you desire to be a mother or because it's expected of women. Does Mom pressure you so she can be a grandma? Does everyone say that you should have a baby? Those reasons are wrong! If being a mom is your number-one desire, consider adopting or having one on your own. Many single women are choosing to get pregnant by a friend or from a sperm bank donation. Andy says, "If you've got the money, be a single mom." Michael McD. agrees:

> 66 You don't need a man to have a child. The best thing is not to try to find someone to fill a void. Everyone has different moral values. If you're looking for a man because your biological clock is ticking and out of time, you'll end doing the wrong thing because you're pressuring yourself. It also may be something you're not ready for, or he may not be ready for. 99

"You don't need to keep hitting your biological clock's snooze button just because there isn't a man in the picture. You've got ninety-nine percent of what it takes to make a baby already and, honey, that other one percent ain't hard to come by."   —Yiannis

As you get older, people stupidly remind you that your window of opportunity for having a baby is decreasing, like you can't figure that out for yourself. That can push you to make poor decisions—marry the "just okay" guy or stay with the jerk for his sperm. If you're single, almost any available man who says he wants kids might seem like the answer. But it's usually not a happy one—for the mom or the child. Ed continues:

" Be thankful your biological clock is still ticking—and RELAX! Or find a nice gay guy willing to 'father.' But be sure to know if it's really 'about having a kid' or if it's really about you being unstable. 'Cuz once that kid comes, if you realize that it wasn't 'about having a kid,' you're screwing up two lives, potentially three (assuming the dad was to be part of it). "

If having a baby is a painful issue, get professional counseling to help you accept that it might not happen. It's unfortunate that life doesn't play out like it does in movies. But, Patrick adds, you must learn to live with the reality that not every woman will meet a man who'll make her happy in time to have kids:

" Seek some professional advice in this department to find out what you really need and want, and whether this is practical. Know yourself and consider whether becoming a single parent would be in the child's best interest. If so, there are a variety of options available to would-be single mothers. Just be careful if you're thinking about asking one of your gay, male chums to help you out in this department. It's a plausible but dicey option that could either strengthen or decimate your friendship. "

Getting a Commitment

Men are often not commitment phobic. They just might not want to commit on your terms. Are you ready for a serious commitment?

Too many women push for it without giving it enough thought on both practical and emotional levels. Before you begin a push to marriage or living together, make sure you've know him long enough to determine he's the man you want to spend your life with. It can take many years to thoroughly know someone. Yet some women push to get married after knowing a guy for months, not years, or pressure him for commitment simply because a certain amount of time has passed. One doesn't just know someone well because a time marker has been reached. Matthew suggests you learn how to slow down and take it easier:

66 Like with a tree, a relationship grows on its own and you have to go along with it. You shouldn't rush into one. It can take two or three or ten years to really get to know somebody. Talk to people who are married for fifty years. They're still getting to know each other. There's a constant rediscovery process, and you've got to naturally let it take its course. You can't try to impose all these artificial constructs around it, such as 'I need to get married after I know him for a year' or 'This is what I expect after dating for two months.' Life does work out. You have to ride it out and see where it goes. Women are always in this huge rush for everything. Men can just hang out and wait. They have a lot more patience than women. Women need to just chill out! 99

"From what I see, almost all men are really on a mission to get married too—so that's good news. Most straight men are kinda helpless and often aimless when it comes to their personal lives."

—Bob

Guys do want to settle down with one woman. But many are very fussy. If he falls in love and thinks she's terrific, he's excited to ask her to share his life. But guys need to get past fears that there might be someone even better around the corner. They often take commitment much more seriously than women do. They're not just looking for a wife. They want to meet special women who can become their wives. But some are never sure that they'll meet a woman they can settle down with. Michael M. clarifies:

> ❝ Commitment is a lifelong problem for a lot of men. There's a mortal terror of commitment and no easy answer. Some guys just want to be able to play the field, and the thought of giving it up is horrifying to them. Women looking for commitment should avoid that type of guy. It's like training a dog: You're never sure they're going to be trained. ❞

If you've been together for a long time and want to make the move, wait until he's in a good mood. Explain what getting to that next level means to you. Emphasize that you want this because you love him, not just because of a schedule. Respect his response. Don't get an attitude if he isn't enthusiastic. Men are scared of commitment for a gazillion reasons. Vinnie suggests:

> ❝ To make him more secure in the relationship, you have to give him space. You also have to realize, though, that he may not decide to commit even after this. Know to move on then, and that it's not a failure. I don't think you can make someone want to be committed. You can make someone feel secure, loved, nurtured,

but you can't make someone want to move onto the next level like on a video game. 🙶🙶

If he's not sure what he wants, agree to wait for a specific period of time with no pressure. Six months to a year is fair. Set a deadline for him to decide if he wants to move forward with you or end it. Be very clear that you can't wait forever and will respect his decision, on the date selected. Once he understands the deadline, don't mention it again.

Give him space to make his decision without pressure. Control your need to know what he's thinking. That's hard! But for your own good, stifle any urges. Don't tell him what he'll lose if he doesn't come around. Leave it alone and enjoy each other. It allows him to think about it and make a rational decision. Michael McD. emphasizes:

🙶🙶 Remember that commitment issues are theirs, not yours. You're not inadequate if he can't commit. Accept that you're not doing something wrong, as some women do. 🙶🙶

Show him by actions why he doesn't want to lose you. Let him experience you without the stress of commitment. Not bringing it up helps him see how delicious you can be. When time is up, ask nicely for his decision. If he says he's not ready, leave quickly and sweetly. Don't tell him off. Express your sadness without getting too emotional. Don't see him again at all. If you have a tender breakup, he may miss you enough to return. Otherwise, be glad you found out. Some men just can't commit.

"If you're dating someone who's commitment phobic and you hang around, my first question would be 'Who's commitment phobic?' Which one of you is more commitment phobic: a guy who's commitment phobic or you, who's hanging around with him?"

—Rick

First-Aid Tips

- Expand your circle of friends so you have more support and people to turn to for fun when you're feeling weak about needing to get married and have kids.

- Write down all the things you think you'll get from being married, other than security, proving yourself to others, or following what you think you should do. Figure out how you can give these to yourself.

- Do something you enjoyed when you were younger but stopped because you were too old for it. Jump rope, visit a zoo, watch *Bambi*, and do other things that remind you of the fun you had then. They can still be lots of fun when you let go.

GOODBYE, DOUBLE STANDARDS

Navigating Sexual Stereotypes to Get More from Men

"The yin and yang of life is you must be naughty and nice to have it all."

—Kevin A.

Men still struggle between what they desire and what they can handle when it comes to a sexual woman. They all desire one who is hot and lament when they're with someone who's not. Yet, when guys do encounter a very sexual woman, many run from her. It's up to you to decide whether to hold back or happily follow your sexuality. If we all decide to own our sexual power in force, men would learn faster to be comfortable with sexual women who communicate, and we'd all smile more.

> "Darling, what you have between your legs is absolutely a sign of gold and power. You must cultivate it, educate it, and activate it. You must use it and turn it out. You can wear it; you can dress."
>
> —Kevin A.

The Eternal Male Conflict

Double standards are confusing and unfair. It's hard for guys to accept that you can be naughty and still be a nice girl. Men crave a whore but feel that a woman they have a relationship with should be a pure, sweet, Madonna type. David says it's confusing for guys to get a balance between thinking with their penises and being logical:

> **"** There's a fine line between it. They want to screw a whore, but don't want to marry her. They want you to look like a prostitute, but not in front of anyone else. It's better to do most of that stuff behind closed doors. He doesn't want anyone else looking at you the way he's looking at you. That's just the way men are. They're possessive by nature, in that sense. Dress sexy, but just for him. Show a little cleavage when you go out for dinner, but make sure to have a jacket or wrap to cover up. Wear lingerie under a nice suit, and take off the suit in front of him. Let him know that you're doing it for him. It's all in your approach. Men love women who are sexy. **"**

It's not wholly a guy's fault if he acts on what he's been taught. Just like our friends create drama by making judgments about men, men discuss the morals of sexual women. Since guys can be chickens about getting into a situation that might make them feel uncomfortable or inadequate, one may have second thoughts about a woman he was just enthralled with after hearing friends negatively analyze women who are open about sex. He may not run, at first. He'll taste and enjoy sex like he never has before. But doubt may ruin things if he can't handle what he wished for. Michael A. explains:

> 66 A sexual woman can undermine a man's role as the dominant force in a relationship. Men are trained to be the powerful ones. You're turning their thinking upside down when you assert your sexuality. And you disorient them because what's down is up and what's left is right. 99

A man may find overt sexuality delicious but wonder if he's satisfying you as much as the men before him, as demons hit—"How many men has she been with?" "What if I can't satisfy her?" "Is she here because she likes me or because she's horny?" Oy! Men can carefully deconstruct the potential for a good relationship by second guessing us, or themselves. What's a sexual girl to do?

> "Follow your instincts. There should be no rules about what you do."   —Kenny

We advise you to do what we've said throughout the book—go slow. Just as you should take it slow out of bed, reveal your sexuality slowly too. Wait until you feel very comfortable before letting a guy see that side of you. Each time a little more trust is earned, he can taste a bit more. If you let it out gradually, it won't overwhelm him. Take your time in general. While double standards make it hard, you should do what feels right for you. Stupid double standards must be broken! Yiannis explains:

66 We still live in a patriarchy, and one of the facets of a patriarchy is to control women's sexuality. A man calling a woman out for sleeping with a guy on the first date when he, himself, would probably attempt to convince you to do the same when on a date with him is no different from straight people calling queers promiscuous and then denying us the right to marry. 99

The Waiting Game

The bad news: Double standards about a sexual woman's morals still exist. The good news: You don't have to follow them. Part of how you're viewed depends on how you view yourself. Feeling a little guilty or on edge about being judged when you follow your sexual desires can attract the reaction you fear. If you feel confident enough to know you have the right to go for yours, it shows. Michael M. says:

66 A lot of guys are attracted to the naughty girls, but then they look down on a woman like that as being of easy virtue. You have to play the naughty and nice cards in succession. Lure them with naughtiness and then show them how nice you are. 99

When you don't worry about what guys think of your sexuality or act like you might be doing something wrong, and when you hold your head up high and do what suits you, things will begin to change.

"If you're out for the night for a good time and you're quick and easy, people react to that. If you go out and feel good and positive about yourself, people won't treat you like you're easy. But have fun too."
—Kevin A.

Before sleeping with a new guy, take into account that many men judge a woman who jumps in early. Of course that's rubbish! He's doing it too. But many men will judge you for it. Whether it's fair or not, it can feel lousy if he disappears after a night of romance, tenderness, and sex. If you're not prepared for that, wait, says Travis:

66 I think it really sucks that there is a double standard. With that said, a lot of women have been taught they need to hold out on sex or treat it like it's something that the guy has to work for. Similarly guys feel like it's a game that they have to win and are trying to get it from you. Personally, I think if a guy coaxes you into having sex with him, it looks like you are caving in and doing it because he wants to. In doing so you are giving him the power. You should know if you want to have sex with a guy, so take the lead or don't let the guy feel like he has won because you slept with him. 99

Have sex when your instincts say it's right for you, not by how many dates you've had. That said, having sex changes the dynamics. If he's a guy who is a potential long-term partner, it's healthier to take it slow. Sex with someone you don't know well can lead to awkwardness afterward. Once you've had sex, your expectations may go way up. At the same time, he may feel more vulnerable and back way off, knowing how women get more serious after having sex. It can get funky pretty quickly if you come on too strong and he goes into his cave, shaking from fear. Kevin S. advises:

66 Take it a little easier if you're into the person. If you want a relationship, you need to slow down. Women can scare men with their come-ons. They shouldn't have it all out at the beginning. Keep it veiled and clouded. When it needs to come off, it'll come off. 99

> "If sex isn't blurring your vision, you can see things a lot more clearly and then decide if this is a person whom you want to be with."   —Kyle

When you make love to a guy you've gotten to know over time, and a friendship is developing, sex is better. So is the dynamic afterward. If he knows the person you are, then there's less judgment. Waiting gives you time to learn how much he already likes you out of bed, so his actions in the sack will feel more real. A guy who's just in it for sex won't stick around for long. And if he does, sex will probably be more about his own pleasure, so you're better off losing him.

"You should hold off on sex for as long as you can. The minute you give it away, he's gone. Men are whores; straight or gay, we're all whores."   —Jason

Go slow afterward too! Be careful about getting too mushy after the first night of sex. That doesn't mean going cold, or even cool. You can sigh, but not too loud. Don't express love or say it was the best. Remember, some men bolt when it feels too good. Show small doses of enthusiasm. While his ego may not like it as much, some nonchalance allows breathing room. He may need to get used to intimacy and reassure himself that he's not trapped now. Hedda advises:

66 A woman should have sex with a man in the first five minutes of meeting a guy if she wants. But she must not cuddle and coo him after the sexual act. Doing such, especially if the sexual act took place in the bathroom of the club you just met in, will make a man feel trapped. She should just pull up her skirt and say, 'Thanks, had a great time,' and leave. He will be so bowled over by this he will pursue her to the ends of the earth. 99

Securing Him in Bed

Many guys act like they have full-blown egos, but they're often insecure puppies and have many issues in bed that plague them. Of course, he won't tell you. He'll act like he's totally fine. If he begins acting weird or questioning you, you'll ask "What's wrong?" and get the standard male response—"Nothing!"

> "Everybody gets insecure about himself or herself in bed. Good God, we're naked!!!!"   —Kevin K.

Since men can't handle their emotions well, and have fewer outlets, they quietly worry inside. Their insecurity often creates fear.

- Insecurity about satisfying you = fear you won't want him as a lover.
- Insecurity about his penis size = fear that you find him inadequate.
- Insecurity about your other lovers = fear that he won't measure up.

Michael McD. points out that men have a lot more feelings than women think and that they're also hampered by double standards:

““ Men have the same concerns that women do—wanting to please. Men want to please women. If one feels he's not pleasing her, he feels insecure. Men are NOT unemotional. Let's not forget that! And women have sex drives. They may not talk about it as much. I think society doesn't accept women having sex drives and doesn't accept men being emotional. That's the problem. There really isn't that much difference between them. ””

Men may not share feelings, but they think about stuff. While they're concerned about whether or not they're satisfying their woman in general, penis size is a big source of insecurity. I asked the guys if men are insecure in bed. Fritz explains that every man worries that you'll find him lacking in inches:

> 66 Everyone always thinks there's gonna be a bigger boy on the block or someone who will last hours longer. I think as much as guys are wrapped up in their sexual organs, they're also very concerned that they don't measure up—that their performance isn't going to be the best. I think guys are all very anxious about that kind of thing. I don't think any straight guy really feels 100 percent confident in that. 99

> "Put your positive thoughts on external speaker. If you think the shape of his penis is beautiful, say it."   —Michael A.

Guys are also scared of not being able to get an erection. We can lie there and fake arousal. He can't fake being hard. You'd be surprised to know how much anxiety men have about not being able to get it up. So how can you make a guy feel better about his member?

While a larger penis might be more visually stimulating, a man who knows how to use his, no matter what his size, can be more satisfying. If he rides you high during intercourse and hits your clit, size won't matter. A small penis makes oral sex easier. Give him a break! Let him know that you love his penis. Tell him it turns you on. Sometimes you have to tell a little white lie to make him feel more comfortable. If he suspects you find him inadequate, he may do stupid things to prove his manhood in other ways. You can't change his basic size, so live with it if you like him and make him feel good about what he has. Patrick agrees but warns not to fake pleasure:

> 66 If applicable, always lie about his penis size. Of course, make sure he's pleasing you. Guide him to your spot and try not to get into the habit of faking orgasms. Your disingenuous moaning will quickly turn to self-parody and self-loathing. If you are truly being pleased, it will be reflected in your partner's confidence level. 99

Men's insecurity comes from many places. Ease his anxieties by being enthusiastic. Instead of saying that "it" feels good, say "YOU make me feel good." Tell him his penis feels wonderful inside, his fingers and tongue drive you crazy. Men love it! Of course, if it doesn't feel wonderful, guide him first so you can be telling the truth.

> "Connect with him in some way mentally, with the eyes, etc. Find what he likes and what you like. And compliment when appropriate."   —Ed

Guys are concerned about what you think. They HATE the thought of being made fun of. Many of us do share all the details. As much as they like to brag, few men who really care about you share intimate details with their buddies. They may say you're hot or like sex or have a good body. But they won't describe your body parts or critique your style. Don't let him know you talk about him in that way with your friends! If you care about your guy, bolster his fragile ego. Find ways to guide him so that everything you say comes true, advises Jason:

> 66 Straight men are much more insecure than gay men. They don't know the woman's body. Ask questions. Sexuality is a very private and intricate thing, and each person has their own thing. You have to be willing to ask questions and to get to know someone on that level. I don't think a lot of people do that. They're too afraid to ask. 99

"They know you judge them and talk to your girlfriends about it!"

—Ed

To Assert, or Not to Assert?
The Question of the Ages

Men complain that women don't make many moves on them. They say they want you to jump their bones—let them know you crave them—have more equality in initiating sex.

Yeah, that's what he says. But when you do it, he gets scared. As we said earlier, men are confused when they get what they say they want. The fantasy of a woman who asserts herself sexually seems so elusive that guys don't know how to react when they actually find one. They like it, explains Fritz, but feel like they're losing control if you try to lead:

> 66 Guys like to feel they're in control, to some degree. You have to be sensitive to how someone reacts to you. If you get a positive response, a green light, go ahead. If he seems to get intimidated, pull back a little. Be aware. 99

"Do what you want. If it feels good, do it. A woman who's really confident should do what she damn well pleases."   **—Andy**

Some men can't help being timid and nervous with a woman who knows what she wants and goes after it. All their insecurities scream at them. You can try to reassure the poor pup, but you must be true to yourself and your needs. We're entitled to be hungry for sex. And a hungry girl should get fed! Michael A. says:

> 66 In the straight community there is no negative word for promiscuity in men. You're a player, but that's actually a good connotation. Being human is about the full expression of your sexual and nonsexual desires. They're not compartmentalized. 99

"You have to be naughtier. Guys play this game, and if the woman realizes that it's just a game, she'll be the one with all the power. You can pretty much do what you want."   **—Kevin A.**

How long do you play coy? A month? Two? How about never? If you stifle your sexuality a lot, men will never learn to accept that women love sex too, and that they should be grateful as heck for it, not critical. The latter's just plain dumb on their parts. Travis agrees:

> ❝ Women need to learn to think like men. The sexiest girl I ever dated—yes, I dated women back in the day—was this girl named Heather. She had the best attitude about sex, dating, and relationships. She talked about it like a man, and it was so awesome to be around a girl who was that cool with it. She wasn't a tomboy or into sports or anything. She was just really with it and wasn't afraid to talk about what she wanted in bed and how that is very different from what she wanted in a relationship. ❞

"A woman shouldn't hold back if she doesn't want to. Sex should be an extension of ourselves—not a replacement!"   —Ed

Gently ease him into getting used to your making sexual moves on him. Flirting gets him used to you being playful and more forward. Gauge his response to that. When you go slowly and wait for him to earn your trust, it's easier to figure out whether he respects you. Does he know what kind of woman you are, or is he still fixated in judgmental schoolboy ways and can't imagine that a woman could be both naughty and nice?

"You have to find out who he is first if you're looking for a relationship. If you don't want one, you want him to do it right and get out."   —Jason

Some men make judgment calls to bury their own insecurities. Men say they don't want to be used for sex either. Deep down, most really want to be liked for themselves, just as we do. They worry that if you want them for sex, that's all you appreciate about them. When the tables are turned, the insecure pups get their silly snouts bent out of shape.

Guys really want to be loved for who they are, even if they think with the wrong head. But it's time they learned that we're entitled to express our desires as much as they do. They also need to get used to nice girls who like to get down and dirty too. Ultimately, it's his problem, not yours. Listen to Michael McD., who says:

66 You don't want to change yourself for anybody. If you need to modify yourself in any sense, other than working on yourself and your issues, then it's not the true you in the relationship. I think being yourself is the most important thing. If someone is going to like you, they're going to like you. It doesn't matter if you're very sexual. Learn how to feel comfortable in your own skin and with your own needs. Find someone who thinks you're perfect the way you are. 99

Many women could run rings around many a man's sex drive and are tired of waiting for him to initiate. What's a horny girl to do? Men and their damn big egos in their pants cause so many problems! While we recommend slowly opening up instead of giving them heart attacks, you eventually must go for yours. Your own perception can affect the way a guy views your sexuality. And if he's not doing it for you or if he's being selfish, it's up to you to set him straight! Matthew elaborates:

> 66 There's a difference between sexual confidence and being a slut. Sexual confidence means you can talk honestly about sex. You can ask him what he's into and not feel you're a slut by asking and not have to keep the whole virgin attitude. A healthy sexual confidence is where you can honestly talk about sexual issues. Guys dig that! 99

> "We should follow our instincts. I'd rather regret something I've done than something I haven't tried."   —Michele

It's okay to slowly ease into your true sexual self to allow time for getting comfortable with each other. But if a guy wants you to always be passive and you want a more active role, let him use his hand on himself while you get outta there! Compromise is best. Respect his need to feel in charge, but teach him by action the benefits of having his own personal horny girl who can't get enough of him. Just be realistic in your expectations, advises David:

> 66 Don't expect him to say 'I love you, I love you' in bed. Let him be the one who takes control and starts things—sort of in charge, at times. If he's the kind of man who can handle you

being more aggressive, then be more aggressive. But he needs to feel like a man in bed. If nowhere else, that's where he needs to feel like a man. If you give a little more, or do a little more to make him feel that way, then do that. It won't kill you, and what you'll be doing will help him be a better lover. **"**

"Naughty is very sexy, and nice is very comforting."   —Rick

When you're comfortable with your sexuality, he'll have no choice but to accept it. Men can handle it if you develop trust before jumping into the sack. When you have friendship in place and a solid foundation, he'll accept a lot more. At that point, he knows who you are, there's hopefully a decent level of communication in place, and he feels more comfortable with you in general. Otherwise, if you're inclined, have sex with someone more casual, and explore yourself first.

First-Aid Tips

- Adopt a pet if you need unconditional love.
- Walk around naked for a day when you're home to get more comfortable with your body and experience the freedom that being clothes free elicits. Then do it with your guy there.
- Practice smiling confidently and force good posture. It makes you feel better about yourself and look stronger when handling his sexual advances.

12

Horny and in Control

How to Take Charge of Your Sexual Desires

"In the past, women were raised to believe that their needs were not important. Women nowadays should tell him what he must do. Send him in the right direction."
—Fritz

Do you wonder how a woman can want to make moves on a guy? Are you in touch with your sexuality? Too many of us have gotten used to suppressing our needs in order to please HIM. It's time to bring the sexual revolution into bed! You can get more comfortable with getting your physical needs satisfied if you choose to. Why settle for half-assed moves while you lie there faking it? Why stifle your sexuality so he doesn't misjudge you? Men aren't the only ones with sex drives! When you give yourself permission to reach your sexual potential, you may smile more. Michael M. says you can change your perception of your role in bed and give yourself permission to experience greater pleasure:

66 Some women are not really raised to be sexual but to be wives, girlfriends, and good girls. There's more shame cloaked around female sexuality than that of males. Men are brought up

to be studs. If a man sleeps around he's a stud; if she does it she's a slut. It's a horrible double standard. Women are taught to be more ashamed of their bodies than men are. Through self-discovery you can learn that it's all baloney and you deserve pleasure in bed. 🙶

Tune into Your Needs

If you begin to let go of stereotypes about sex, you can focus on all those warm, tingly feelings that can explode into a profusion of pleasure when you loosen up. You can unlearn any tales you've been taught and become a smiling, sexual being in control of her sexuality. The guys and I will tell you how. It starts with YOU getting comfortable with YOU. Michael McD. stresses that it's important to accept that sex is not a dirty thing:

🙶 It's hard for many women to feel comfortable about sex. I think even now that many women would feel very dirty if they had a one-night stand. You feel as if you're being used. These women don't feel very good about themselves. It comes back to society's programming that sex outside of marriage or a relationship is bad. Women have to stop viewing sex like that. Everyone enjoys it. Having sex outside of a relationship doesn't make you bad. You have needs to fulfill, like everyone else. It doesn't make you a slut. 🙶

Sex is fun, yummy, and worth having and having. And having. You're entitled to enjoy your sexuality, no matter what he or Mom or the media says. When something feels good, let him know. The closer you get to your guy, the more you can develop intimacy that allows you to feel freer to express your desires. Rick advises taking responsibility for communicating your sexual desires:

66 If you don't know what you want in bed or won't tell your guy, it's just another way to avoid responsibility. When you are intimate enough with somebody, a dialogue can be very sexy. Talk about what you want and like. You don't have to do it, but talk about it first. You can get a good impression of someone by talking about what you want and like by whether or not it turns him on. You talk about your sexual desires and what you like to do—that's really hot. It's a delicious combination. 99

Clueless in Bed?

Do you complain about his lovemaking skills or lack of them? If you're not getting the satisfaction you want, it's time to guide him. As clueless as men can be in general, they take it to another level in bed. He may not know what you want him to do because you, and probably women before you, didn't tell him.

In straight relationships, men learn about women from women. Unless you're lucky enough to have a guy who was trained well by a former girlfriend, you'll have to find ways to let him know how to satisfy you. That's much better than faking pleasure and complaining to friends about what a lousy or selfish lover he is. If you don't like what he does, do something! Mike urges:

❝ You'll never be pleased if you don't express yourself in bed. Men can't read minds, but it's not all about telling with words. The way you move and moan says a lot. ❞

"Most men aren't smart enough to know when they're bad in bed. It's remarkable how the male brain can thoroughly convince the man it belongs to that women reach orgasm from making their men happy."   —Michael T.F.

Since we're better at complaining than at gently guiding a lover, men don't understand a woman's body as much as we'd like. Many of us don't understand it either, so we take what we get. Why settle for crumbs when you can have a yummy meal? Go for the whole enchilada in bed, says Michael McD.:

❝ Don't be passive-aggressive! For instance, if you enjoy being orally pleased, don't physically push his head. Let him know what you enjoy. Communicating what you want in bed comes with feeling comfortable talking about sex in an intimate way. A lot of problems are caused by a lack of healthy communication. People often communicate poorly, so they come off the wrong way. ❞

"Read a sex manual together. Bookmark the pages you want to review together, then, like good students, practice, practice, practice!"   —Randall

Do you think that guys are all alike? Just let him inside of your vagina, or rub him up and down or suck him, and he'll orgasm on cue? NOT! Different men like different ways of being handled. Of course, any touch will do something for him. But why not learn what he likes best? How? Ask him, or listen carefully to his response when you stimulate him in different ways. Alex explains:

66 Every man is unique. What might be pleasurable for one might not do it for the next. That's where communication comes into play. Ask your man to tell you exactly what he likes. Also, women need to recognize the difference between circumcised and uncircumcised men. It's a completely different technique. What feels good on a circumcised man may be torture on an uncircumcised one. Uncircumcised men are usually more sensitive than circumcised ones are. Fine-tune each other to maximize each other's pleasure. Otherwise you may do something generic that won't quite do it for him. Come up with a customized technique that does wonders for your partner. 99

Tell Him How You Like Sex

Too many women allow a guy they're involved with to believe that if he's not criticized, he's doing a good job. If you fake orgasms, he happily deludes himself that's he's got the goods and is using them effectively. It's your responsibility to educate him about your body. Don't expect him to know on his own. While some people have more instincts than others, no one is born with the ability to read minds. And while every woman is different, guys stick to what they think worked before if they're not set straight. How can you get better pleasuring from him in bed? Michael A. has a technique that he says makes it easier to communicate:

> ❝ Use what I call a 'foreplay forum.' Get naked, hold each other and complete the following sentences. I love it when you do ____. It really turns me on when you do ____. I want to turn you on more. What is it that you want me to do? It really comes down to communication, but it helps when you're naked. ❞

To continue to get your point across, Michael M. adds:

> ❝ Instead of putting the guy down by saying 'Don't do that, do this,' you have to encourage your partner by saying 'That's great. Now how about trying this?' So it becomes a positive exploration that you do together, like a joint adventure. Negative comments can be very negative to a sex life. ❞

If you're comfortable with him, have a friendly chat when you're not in bed. Emphasize that you love sex with him and can envision it getting even hotter. Ask if there are things he'd like to try. Casually mention what you'd love him to try. If you desire something but don't know how he'll react to an overt suggestion, say you read about it and it turned you on to think about doing it with him, and with a twinkle in your eye ask if you can try it for real. Alex advises carefully choosing how you state your case:

     " It's all in how you word it. Don't ever say things like 'You're not satisfying me like this.' Be more gentle with men when they're sensitive. Use an approach like 'Honey, put your hands here. I like it when I'm touched this way.' Be open about it. It could help if you discussed it while not having sex. During sex can put on pressure. I don't think sitting down to discuss what each likes would be crazy at all. If you can't have that kind of conversation with each other, communication goes down the drain. **"**

The longer you wait before having sex, the more comfortable you can become with each other. The longer you get to know him as a person, the better your chance of creating a connection that results in having more satisfying interactions once you get between the sheets. Since communication is key both in and out of bed, practice it!

"Find out where your comfort zone is. Talk about it when you're not having sex. You need to relax. Each guy is different. Ask a lot of questions. Communicate. Make it sexy and fun."   **—Jason**

We don't know nearly what we could about pleasing a guy, but we can find out. The guys are particularly helpful here since they have male bodies. Differences between men and women can come out in bed but shouldn't be a problem if you understand them. Let him know what you like in a positive way. If you work together (not you doing the work for him or expecting only him to change) you can find ways to compromise with the differences, Alex says:

> 66 I think that men need to learn how to be more expressive, and women can help them do that—to be more expressive about what they like. Learn as you go along if a man likes to have his ears nibbled or if he likes to have his nipples touched. 99

Whose Orgasm Is It?

You feel an orgasm rising. You've allowed yourself to relax and enjoy his stimulation. Oooooo, it feels so good. And then, booof—he breaks the momentum by asking if you're almost there. Good-bye, orgasm! In an instant, his question broke your concentration. Now you're self-conscious, knowing that he's waiting for you to climax, so you fake it and stifle the anger at being deprived of a real one. Don't let him get away with that! There is so much more to sex than just having an orgasm. Rick explains:

> 66 There are too many aspects of a sexual experience to just focus on one. It's like a guy going to the gym because he wants to be huge and muscular. He takes all this testosterone so he can be huge, but then all his hair falls out. Experience all of sex. An orgasm is just one part. It's not the entire experience. Take the time to smell the roses. There's a whole garden down there that you'd be missing out on. 99

"When a man focuses on trying to give an orgasm, it's like trying to hit a bull's-eye."   —Brian

Do you get anxiety when your guy is waiting for your orgasm? It's admirable if he truly wants to please you, but many men treat a woman's orgasm like it's the target of a game he's trying to score in. Knowing that his ego needs to achieve success can deflate any chance of actually climaxing. It's hard enough for many of us to get there, without him adding pressure. That can motivate an obligation to fake. Vinnie warns that when you do this, he gets the pleasure of thinking he gave you an orgasm, and you feel cheated:

66 You don't want to get two years into a relationship and all of a sudden divulge 'You've never given me an orgasm!' I think there's nothing wrong with faking it once in a while, though, especially at the beginning when it's just awkward anyway. 99

"A woman should only fake an orgasm if she wants it to be over."   —Rick

Are you scared he'll leave if you don't give him what he expects? Some men do leave or make you feel inadequate if he can't get you off quickly. And we buy it. That's such crap! He doesn't learn to give you what you need, and you reward him by faking. How unfair is that?!? VERY. You're not a failure if you don't climax on cue.

If a lover asks if you came yet, ask what he expects you to say when he's looking at you expecting to hear you had an orgasm. Those questions push women to fake. You need to speak up, but gently. Be clear that he shouldn't take it personally and that women just have a different mentality about orgasms. Mike explains:

> For many men, it's a machismo thing, making sure he pleases you, which is not a bad thing in a guy, considering so many don't care. If it's a problem, let him know that, and assure him that it does not mean anything to his masculinity.

"Take an entrepreneurial attitude about sexuality."

—Michael McD.

If your guy really wants to satisfy you, tell him not to focus on your orgasm, like that's all sex is. Many of us don't always need an orgasm to be satisfied. It's better if he asks if you want more stimulation. Just as important—learn to give him prompts as he stimulates you. Tell him what feels good. Encourage him to keep doing something you love. Often he asks because you're lying there in silence and he can't tell what you like. Open up more and be clear about what you like, whether you verbalize it out of bed or prompt him with groans and encouragement during sex. Michael A. advises:

> The only way to put the 'ohh' back in orgasm is to remove the expectation of having it. You can't 'try' for an orgasm any

more than you can 'try' to sweat or go to sleep. So have an honest conversation and tell him he's putting too much pressure on you. Oddly, the best way to have an orgasm is to stop trying for one (very Zen, isn't it?). So get him to agree that for the next month or so you aren't 'allowed' to have an orgasm. That'll take the pressure off both of you and free you to focus on feelings, sink into sensations, and pay attention to pleasure. Which, oddly enough, is the footpath to orgasms. **"**

Sex for One

The best way to nurture great sex is to learn about your own body. Unfortunately, many of us are not in tune with our own bodies and expect him to figure it out. While men can be clueless, we contribute to it. They assure me that they want to please. But how can they improve without guidance? When a guy asks his lady what she likes, MANY say "everything." What they really mean is DUH! If you don't know what you like, how can you tell him? Many women wait for a guy to figure it out. Please accept that in order to know how to guide your guy to please you, you have to learn to please yourself. David says that there's no way to communicate what feels good and what you like if you don't know, since knowing your body is your own responsibility:

" It's not somebody else's job to do it for you. Single or involved, you should be able to take care of yourself sexually. There may be times when you want an orgasm and he may not be around for a day or two. So pull out your friend or take a nice sudsy bath. Find out what it feels like to feel good and to have an orgasm so when you're in bed with somebody you know what it feels like. Then if you're in bed and he's not helping you get there, you know how to help him. 🢒🢒

Men are always shocked about how many women don't give themselves orgasms. Try to keep his hands off his penis and fight a losing battle. Men make friends with their member at a young age. It's natural. They touch it many times a day for practical purposes. Eventually they discover it gets hard, and if they rub it they experience a pleasurable ejaculation. Most of us don't just wake up one morn with an urge to touch our vaginas. If you've been brought up to keep your vagina clean and that's it, you may not discover that touching brings pleasure. Your sexuality evolves by getting to know your own body. Fritz says:

🢐🢐 I had a girl here a few years ago who was being instructed by the other girls on my staff on the art of self-pleasure. This is something that she in her thirties had never done. If you don't know what feels good for yourself, how will you tell someone else? Don't be afraid to look after yourself. Everyone's own needs are very important. 🢒🢒

"There's nothing wrong with masturbation. It doesn't hurt anybody. I think women learn—'What the hell, I'm not going to go blind.' It's the ultimate victimless crime."   —Michael M.

Many women thanked me for the chapter in *All Men Are Jerks Until Proven Otherwise* on how to pleasure yourself. You can masturbate any time and with a guy too.

Doing it gives you sexual power—you can guide him to better sex, help yourself have an orgasm during sex, stay strong about not jumping into bed with the wrong guy, and not stay with one if you can satisfy your own urges. Brian agrees that pleasuring yourself is good for you:

66 Practice makes perfect. I think it's good to enjoy touching yourself. Like a good car, you have to keep it tuned up. 99

"The more we know about ourselves, the more we can give."
—Michele

If you don't pleasure yourself, please try. Don't wait for a guy to open you up. Do that yourself so your sex life is active with or without a partner. Find a private time, get some lubricant and maybe a vibrator. Make love to yourself in private. Learn to enjoy it as a separate pleasure from sex with a guy—one that keeps on giving—literally. Kevin A. reminds you:

66 You must know yourself. That's what God gave you. You must be with yourself and touch yourself. We're all like mazes, and no one can figure it out but you. 99

"I think every woman should own a vibrator and masturbate whenever it occurs to her."   —Vinnie

Horniness can definitely warp our brains too, so own your sexual power and stay out of sexual trouble with your vibrator! Orgasms are there for your taking. Don't depend on HIM for them. He'll benefit from it too when your sexuality heightens! Rick has a suggestion for keeping yourself from making poor decisions about having sex with a guy you're not sure of:

66 I think masturbation and any form of self-pleasure are great ideas before a date. This way your sex urge won't cloud your decision making. You're able to see things more clearly, and you won't be focused on getting off because you already have. You'll be able to see what else this person has to offer other than what he has between his legs. It totally defines an untapped treasure. 99

Stop Thinking So Much!

Too often we don't lose ourselves in bed because we think too much. Am I clean enough? Does he like my scent? Am I doing it right? Are my thighs jiggling too much? Will my cellulite turn him off? Is he enjoying what I'm doing? Yada, yada, yada!! If you really want to enjoy sex, you need to relax about all those things that men don't even notice when they're turned on. Kyle reveals:

" When men are having sex, they think the same way they always do—with their penises. Trust me! There's only one thing on their minds, and it's not your cellulite and imperfections. "

We think too much during sex. How can you have a great time if worrying keeps you from getting lost in it? If you want to experience ecstasy in bed, give your mind a rest! Be in the moment. Don't think about what went wrong last time or what future potential you have with him. Think about how good his touch feels. How delicious it is to have your guy inside you. How nice he tastes and feels. Period!

"Have a glass of wine. That relaxes everybody. Let him see everything. Let him know right from the start what your likes and dislikes are."   —Jason

Confidence is a big elixir for both sexes. When you act confidently with your guy, his attention is on your attitude. Guys can't pay attention to more than one thing at a time. If you've captured him with a sexy confidence, he won't notice dimples on your butt, unless you point them out. When you bare yourself to a guy, there's always a bit of vulnerability in the mix. But confidence keeps it from turning to insecurity. Quiet the voices in your head, suggests Alex:

" Those voices are as empty as some guys' minds can seem at times. Everybody has insecurities. You need to be comfortable enough with your partner so that it doesn't become an issue. Talking about it is very important. You might be surprised how insecure your partner also is. 🙶🙶

"I call the voices in your head 'The Committee.' They're very bossy. You can listen to them but shouldn't acknowledge them. They'll always be there. Put them on mute."   —Jason

What's on your mind? A jiggly butt? What position makes you look thinner? If you worry, you'll never fully lose yourself in passion and pleasure. Furthermore, is he perfect when naked? I doubt it. Often we're too obsessed with our own imperfections to notice or care about his. Most guys don't worry about having a bit of flab or too much hair or skinny legs or a flat butt. When I tell them how women worry about what men think of their bodies, they're shocked and laugh. If he's with you, he's attracted to you. During sex, he's most likely only thinking about what you're doing to him.

In Chapter 14 we'll tell you how to make yourself feel more beautiful and develop better self-esteem. That makes it easier to silence fears. So does getting comfortable with a guy before getting naked. When you know he likes you for who you are, lighten up. Once you allow passion to control your thoughts, you'll be more receptive to what he does. Communication flows to another level when you guide him on autopilot because you're too aroused to think straight. One of the sexiest things you can do is confidently strut around naked in front of him. Men love it! If he sees your body à la carte, he won't complain, despite flabby thighs, butt, and tummy, dimples and all. Kevin S. advises:

" Put yourself out there sexually. You should be thinking about your personal pleasure. What pleasure are you taking from sex? It is a mental hang-up. We don't get younger, thinner, and more beautiful. You can look at the external. It's all emotional inside. He's in bed with you, and you're going to have doubts now? It's time to turn it on and please yourself. "

Relax and Enjoy

Would you use the word *fun* to describe sex? It should be when you're comfortable with your partner, and yourself. Sex is too much fun to give it the heavy overtones that some women attach to it. Ed recommends:

" Sex can be a wonderful playground that allows you to experience feelings and emotions that you cannot experience in very many ways. Enjoy the sexual experience! A lot of people are taught that it's only for "procreation," but I STRONGLY disagree. HAVE FUN WITH IT! It's a wonderful stress releaser and can be a wonderful expression of love with the right person. "

Kevin S. adds:

" You need to loosen up. If you're not having fun in bed, you're doing something wrong, mentally or physically, or you're not doing enough of something. He's in bed with you. It's your time. Have fun! If you need to dress up in a costume, whatever. You have to jump on your sexual moment. The more timid you are about sex, the more timid you're going to become about sex. **99**

Good sex is not about him and not about you. It's about the interaction between both of you. If you just wanted an orgasm, you could do it yourself. When you care about each other, giving pleasure is such fun! So is receiving. A good combo rocks! Michele advises that you should expect to receive lots of pleasure too:

66 A real man/gentleman wants his woman to enjoy the sexual act as much as him—or even more. I know some men don't care, but who cares about them! A woman has to understand that he's there for her—relax, let him play, and play with him. **99**

Get lost—in his touch, his scent, his mouth. Many women don't. Tap into your sensuality. There are many little things that you can do that will drive him mad with little effort. Lose yourself in the interaction. A gay friend told me that a big difference between gay and straight lovers is that women often look up when they're going down—they need to know that the guy is enjoying her sucking. Most gay guys don't care. They're too wrapped up in what they're doing to think about it. Try to lose yourself in him. If you let your guy know how much you enjoy pleasuring him, he'll love it. Encourage him to express his pleasure too. Curt suggests:

❝ Feel out how your partner is reacting to everything you do, and then play off of that. Tell him to be vocal in the process and let you know how you're doing. Ask what his most sensitive parts are. Let yourself go. It should come naturally. If you learn to let go and communicate on a different level, it will happen. You have to let go of all your worries and all your beliefs. Sex is very erotic if there are no boundaries. Nothing's wrong or right. ❞

Silence can create insecurity. Moan—for real. Don't act. It's much more fun when the purrs and groans come without trying, because you're so aroused. When you hear your partner respond-ing, and he hears you, it can motivate you more to continue. The more noise you make, the more he's spurred to lose himself in pleasing you. Here's a surprising fact about men from Alex:

❝ Men immediately wonder what you're thinking [when you are too quiet]. That's when insecurities come in. It can convey bore-dom and send many mixed messages. You should be expressive and communicative. You should never fake it. Allow yourself to indulge in feeling the right to feel this pleasure just as men can, and be expressive about it. Let yourself go however it manifests itself. You don't have to be loud, but don't hold back. Enjoy it. ❞

Often we're quiet if we've never felt comfortable letting go with expressions of pleasure. Self-consciousness can stifle emotions during sex, even in women who are expressive out of bed. Many men are silent, so you might not know it's okay to moan out loud.

Holding feelings in can start with being scared that a roommate or neighbor will hear you. Then keeping quiet becomes a habit. Sometimes silence happens because sex just isn't pleasurable enough to stimulate moans. Once you learn what arouses you, teach him and slowly express your delight. Tell him how good he makes you feel. Allow the sensations to turn into noises that express how much you like them.

One factor that can enhance sex is physical fitness. Studies show that exercise raises endorphins, increases energy, and improves body image. Being in better physical shape allows for more variety in positions and greater longevity during sexual play. Working out together can be a BIG turn-on. Go to the gym together, and jump each other's bones as soon as you get home. Patrick agrees:

> ❝ Remember, if you're both sedentary, chances are you're not going to be very motivated to have intercourse. Seek out opportunities to become physically active together. Nothing inflames physical passion more than shared physical exertion—a hike, an hour at the gym, vigorous gardening, a game of nude Twister, etc. In the same regard, nothing is more of a turnoff than the appearance of a slothful, sedentary partner. ❞

And don't forget to be playful with your partner. The best sex partner is often someone you can laugh with. Feeling uptight takes the fun away. Clear your mind and focus on what's going on NOW. Give yourself permission to rock him and be rocked (more on this in the next chapter).

First-Aid Tips

- Buy yourself something pretty in a sensual fabric and enjoy feeling sexy solo.
- Take responsibility when you choose to have sex. Decide if you're ready to take things to the next level and if you can handle it if he doesn't share your feelings and leaves afterward. If you're not, wait until you know him better and use your vibrator.
- Explore a sex shop or catalog. Buy something fun that's not lingerie.

ROCK HIS WORLD—AND YOURS—IN BED

Pointers for Heating Up Sex

*"Instead of thinking you should try everything once,
be open to trying everything three times."*

—*Fritz*

Sex with a caring partner makes you want to do whatever you can to please him. I asked the guys to share their best, hottest, most instructive tips for rocking your guy's world in bed. Get Chapter 12 down first so your world is rocked too. Learning how to please your guy can bring you enough benefits to make reading this chapter worth it.

When you become the lover of his dreams, you're more likely to enjoy your own reality—he'll be even happier to please you in bed, and may even do extra chores. Open your mind and get more creative.

"Sex is as much emotional and mental as it is physical. Surprise your man, and your rewards will be many." —**Randall**

Try the Whole Menu

There's much more to sex than missionary intercourse and genital stimulation. Be open-minded if you want to enjoy sex to the max. Try some new things at least once. You never know! If he suggests something out of the ordinary for you, honor that by not having a bad reaction. You have a right to turn him down. But give him the right to ask without a fuss. A guy shows trust when he suggests something. Be open-minded! David adds:

66 Never make him feel like he's weird or a freak for wanting to try different things. If you really care about him, try everything that he wants to try. You know what? You may like it. But if you don't, you don't. The truth is, if you don't satisfy him he'll be satisfied sexually somehow. It would be better if you're the one doing it. That's the way men are. Be willing to be spontaneous. I always tell girls, 'Be his freak!' 99

While not all men will cheat if you don't keep them happy, intimacy and sex are important for a relationship to grow. If you're with him for the long haul, or want to be, variety keeps sex fresh. Many couples say that sex gets better as you grow together, learn about each other's body and needs, and feel comfortable communicating and exploring together. Try different positions. Read other books for info about specific angles and techniques. For example, when a man enters you when your legs are close together, with either him on top or you, you have the best chance of reaching an orgasm. But since every woman is different, try it all.

"Get into role-playing games. Use different outfits; take it slower and go different places. Be creative."   —Jason

Approach sex like a pupu platter—a taste here, a bite there, and you'll find lots of nibbles you like. Intercourse from the rear has the best chance for hitting your G-spot and allows him or you to stimulate your clitoris by hand. It can be extremely arousing, yet many women don't like this less intimate position. Some women think it means the guy isn't into you, but that's so not true! It can feel impersonal since you can't kiss or make eye contact when you're not facing each other. Or you may worry he'll notice your imperfect bum. Trust me, he'll only notice pleasure. Rear-entry intercourse creates cellulite blindness in most men. Return to missionary position before orgasm so you can end more romantically. Talk about this out of bed so no one's feelings get hurt during sex. If you'd like something, ask carefully, so he doesn't feel inadequate about pleasing you. You can communicate without trashing his ego. David advises:

66 After you've had sex a couple of times and it's not doing it for you, initiate different things on your own. If you like being on top, say 'Honey, can wo try this?' Roll him over and do it the way you like it. Show him—he's going to love pleasing you. A man wants to please a woman in bed. That makes him feel good, makes him feel like a man. So if he's not pleasing you, figure out a way to get him to, and make him feel like he did it. You're gonna need to do some juggling on your side. Whatever it is he isn't doing, let him know. 99

Communication and trust need to be developed for the most awesome sex possible. THIS IS NOT JUST FOR HIM, LADIES! Why not get your world rocked in bed too? This can take time— another reason to go slow. In this chapter we suggest ways to create pleasure in bed. Try some. If stuff is new to you, set boundaries before you begin. Establish that he'll stop if you ask him to. You can't know how something will feel until you've tried it, no matter what your imagination conjures. Further, Glenn says:

““ When you find what your partner likes and he knows what you like, you can go at it and satisfy each other. That leaves less reason to cheat. 🙹🙹

> "Trust has to build in so many other aspects of the relationship. From there, you can form trust in each other sexually as well."
> —Alex

Learn the difference between sexual and sensual. Nurture your sensual Goddess. Sensual is a mood, an attitude, a touch, a reaction. When you work on that in yourself, it puts you more in the mood too Sex isn't just about stimulating genitals. Arousal on many levels leads to the best sex. Use your hands to caress his whole body. It all adds to the sensuality. Be aware that even men need sensual stimulation. Don't take it personally if he needs a lot. Try new things! Matthew observes:

66 When I see straight people having sex in movies it looks horrible. It looks as boring as doing laundry to me. So be creative! You don't even have to have intercourse. It takes the burden off men feeling like they have to follow a script or play a role. Come at it from a more playful angle. Guys are more playful than women are. Women have to play more and make it more fun. Take off the onus of it having to be a certain way. Be ready to experiment more. 99

"Try everything. If you don't like it, don't do it again. But if you don't try it, you'll never know. There's a world of stimulation awaiting you."   —Fritz

Men may seem to only want the overt sexual acts, but they respond very well to sensual stimulation. Very well. They may not know it because few women seem to do it. But if you let him lay back and kiss him gently, just brush his lips with yours, softly blow when you kiss, he'll heat up. Then just graze your lips across other body parts—his eyes, face, shoulders, ears, neck, chest, tummy, and so on. Every inch of the body can be an erogenous zone if you make it one. Whisper something sexual in his ear. Curt explains:

66 The magic of touch is so important. And kissing. I think you can communicate and not say one word but just kiss. You can do so many wonders for each other just by kissing. Also, look in each other's eyes. I think that sort of connection is a very powerful act of intimacy. 99

Men may always be in the mood, but sensual touch and kisses and expressing your feelings can take his craving for you to a new level. And if this is a guy you're in love with, who's earned your trust over time, you can make it even better! Curt advises:

❝ If you're really into the person, during your climactic moment, tell him how much you love him. I think that is the most powerful tool. When you tell him that you love him, that moment is magic. It's a gift you're giving him and he's giving you. I think you should concentrate on pleasing your partner instead of being pleased, because if you're with the right person, you will be pleased too. **❞**

"We love touch as much as you do. Our skin is just as sensitive, maybe more so."   **—Mike**

Orally Loving His Southern Head

Most of the guys emphasized that oral sex is the best way to rock his world. If a guy feels powerless at work, oral sex can soothe him. While getting it, they feel like they're the kings—the center of attention—and all pleasure giving is directed at them. It can be a power trip. The guys agree that many heterosexual men consider oral sex to be the gold standard of sexual expression. It communicates that a woman is into him. Hedda says:

66 This piece of advice was passed down from my mother Shredda Lettuce, who heard it from her mother Bedda Lettuce: Blowjob! If done right it is quick and easy and involves very little effort. It is all about hand and mouth coordination and can take as little as four minutes to accomplish. Besides, it makes a man feel so special. 99

> "Whether you like it or not, guys like it when you go downtown."
> —Fritz

Why are blowjobs so important to men? For many reasons, say the guys. It's a visual thing for many men who love to watch their lady's head going up and down. Some men prop themselves up to watch you inhale his manhood. They love it more when they see enthusiasm, but any oral attention down south is worth watching and considered sexy. Since so many women balk at oral sex, if you go down men are ecstatic. When you're giving it, he feels truly like "the man." It also makes him feel like you care more. For many men, oral sex is the ultimate of great sex. Curt elaborates:

66 It's a power thing. Oral sex feels good, yes, but the under-lying meaning is a manipulative feeling. He's making her do some-thing for him. Also, men like the fact that she is going to that level for him. 99

We can't emphasize enough how much you'll please your guy by giving oral sex. Any mouth-to-penis contact will delight him. Even if you suck his southern half clumsily, even without enthusiasm, it's a gift. If you want to give him the jackpot, show some enthusiasm while doing it. Some women say they like giving their guy pleasure, but few say they love sucking his penis. Yet MANY guys say they get tremendous pleasure giving us oral sex. It can be uncomfortable and tiring. But if you're with a guy you sincerely care about, think of his penis as the most important extension of himself, like he does, and revere it. Make love to it as you would his lips. David explains:

> 66 A lot of women don't want to give head. Oral sex is very important to men. If you don't know how to do it, there are parties where a person comes to a group of friends and shows you how to give head properly. Be willing to try something that you don't want to do, with enthusiasm. 99

The guys warn there are things to be aware of when giving head. Straight men complain that women hurt them by not being careful with those choppers used to chew food. This is one kind of meat to keep your teeth away from! Curl your lips over your teeth before going down. Practice. It's not hard and makes a huge difference in how much pleasure he gets. Sucking his penis with teeth biting or scraping adds pain to the pleasure. Michele adds:

> 66 When it comes to blowjobs, the more you can get into your mouth without him feeling your teeth, the better. 99

"Gagging isn't attractive. So practice on whatever's handy: a banana, a carrot, or the UPS guy."   —Randall

Michael A. has a tip for making oral sex more pleasurable for your guy:

66 The most important thing is to keep your mouth lubricated. Make your mouth a saliva factory. Imagine biting into a lemon. A neat little trick is put the tip of your tongue to the back of your throat for ten seconds. You'll feel the saliva pool at the bottom of your mouth. The most important thing physically is to have a lot of saliva in your mouth. Heat and moisture are what make it feel good. 99

Have water nearby and take a drink before you start sucking him. Both the hand and mouth can participate, so put saliva on your hand or use an edible lubricant to make your hand or mouth nice and slippery. Anticipation makes a big difference. Many of the guys recommend you begin sucking slowly and build his excitement in increments. Don't be in a rush. As he gets worked up, go a little faster. You can also ask if he wants you to speed up. Use your hand and mouth on his penis while he still has his underwear on. Once the anticipation builds, it's hard to do anything that he won't like. Michael A. advises:

66 Start at the outer perimeter and work your way in. It's always better to work your way in than to work your way out. That creates

anticipation, triggering all kinds of neurochemicals and heightening sensations. The best way to begin oral sex is manually. Touch, tease, and play. You want to create a sense of anticipation. One great technique is, with his underwear on, blow hot air to his testicles, through the underwear. It's an amazing feeling —very sensual. It's a preview of what's to come, like coming attractions. **99**

Lick his penis up and down. Use your mouth on the sensitive top region and your tongue on the ridge in front. Experiment with other ways. His response will guide you. Give him variety. The guys agree that you should lick him up and down, in circular movements around the shaft, and any combo you can think of. Some men prefer stimulation around the base. The preferred speed and pressure vary among guys. So ask! He'll let you know if he wants it faster or harder. Many men are so happy to get oral sex that they aren't too fussy. Make yours great—he'll notice and appreciate you for it! Mike says:

66 Use more touching around the penis and tongue around the top. You've got to excite all the nerves! It's not just the shaft. Make it a whole body experience. And hey, try slipping a finger in the back door too while you're down there and see what he thinks! **99**

"You're not at Nathan's and it's not a hotdog! Eat it gently. Go at it softly. No biting."   —Glenn

Use your hand along with your mouth to help maintain your stamina for giving good head. Start at the base of the penis and let it go up and down with your mouth so you don't have to go too deep. Go up and down with your hands and your mouth. Give attention to the testicles while you're sucking and licking. They're often ignored during sex, but they shouldn't be! Gently, ladies! Lick them, kiss them, and suck them carefully. They're sensitive. Teeth should not even be near them! The testicles need to be treated with loving care. Michael M. emphasizes:

> **"** The testicular sack is part of the whole package. Be very gentle. Licking is better than sucking. Sucking can hurt. You'd be amazed at how easily a guy can be in pain from something that's supposed to be pleasurable. But it's different for each person. **"**

Use your fingers on the testicles too. If you give his genitals the royal treatment, he'll probably reciprocate a lot more. Many of the guys recommend licking and tickling the place between the butt and scrotum called the taint. It's a very sensitive spot, and if you stimulate it without too much pressure, you can take him to another level of pleasure. Travis agrees that multitasking during oral sex gets more bang for the suck:

> **"** Oral sex is awesome, but don't forget to use your hands. Stroke him while you are sucking and play with his balls. Also, don't be afraid to lick his balls—none of my girlfriends ever did that, and boy did they miss out on a good thing! **"**

"Oral sex should always be reciprocal. If you're doing that for him, he should do it for you."   —David

Men like you to swallow. Most women don't want to. Ask him to let you know when he's about to get off, and keep your head on the inner side of his wand. Switch to just using your hand as he begins to erupt. At that point, most guys won't know the difference. Keep your head going up and down in rhythm with your hand.

If you're really into the guy, try to get used to his taste (which can be affected by his diet, by the way). If possible, keep a towel or tissue nearby to drop his load in (without him seeing), especially if it's in your hand instead of your mouth. And if cum does get into your mouth, NEVER make a production of spitting it out. Men HATE that. It's part of them and they want to feel that you like it. Nobody wants to feel that a part of him disgusts his lover. Most women don't care for swallowing it, so don't feel guilty if you're one of them. But be subtle about any repulsion you may feel. Quietly let it ooze into a towel or tissue. Then go to the bathroom and rinse your mouth if it bothers you.

"Swallowing probably has to do with a male's complete and total desire for dominance, like truly planting his seed. It doesn't matter if it doesn't grow in your throat, as long as he's planted it."

—Rick

Learn to appreciate the joy of orally pleasuring a guy you're crazy about. Get rid of old hang-ups or bad memories of tediously sucking or feeling squeamish. While men try to ignore it, they do know when you have these feelings, and it bothers them. Don't you just hate it when a guy gets yucky about going down on you? Same thing! Nobody, not a man or a woman, wants to feel that his genitals put his partner off. So if it's really distasteful, be an actress, please! You may learn to enjoy it.

It's fine to expect him to be clean. Take a shower with him first to ensure that he's nice and fresh! Even if you never love it, you can make peace with his southern regions. If he thinks you enjoy it, his pleasure will be increased—a lot. Use the tips we offered for giving head. If you can lose yourself in his penis, he'll love you like you've never been loved before.

Nipple Nookie

Do you think of nipple stimulation as something for women only? It's not! Many straight men don't know that their nipples are sensitive. But those who've experienced it know how good nipple stimulation feels. Randy has educated many straight girlfriends on how to stimulate a straight man's nipples. He suggests:

66 Take time to turn on your man by exploring the most neglected area of the male body—the nipples. Not every guy has sensitive nipples, but plenty do and are waiting for the right woman to introduce them to the joys of nipple jobs. Test your

man's boundaries first with some gentle licking or nibbling to make sure he's OK with nipple play. If he looks happy, start experimenting. Your goal is to increase the sensitivity of his nipples, and there are four main ways to do that—licking, blowing, sucking, and nibbling. Try those steps in that order and watch his face and body. If he moans, shakes, or shivers, you're on to something. Once your man is having a good time, mix things up, making sure he can't see what's coming next. **"**

Some guys may balk or wonder what you're doing. But many will appreciate finding another arousal technique. Some who are resistant to having their nipples stimulated go crazy when you actually do it. Everyone is different. But it's worth a try. Sometimes men like their nipples played with during a blowjob. Lick your fingers or get a drop of edible lubricant before playing with his nipples. Randy adds:

" Suck, lick, suck, nibble. Blow, suck, lick, lick, nibble! If you're comfortable with the idea, bite down a bit harder as you nibble, making sure to watch his reaction carefully so you don't go too far. Some guys enjoy gentle nipple play, while others like it rough; your job is to find his pleasure zone. Remember to go back and forth between nipples. If he's reaching a form of rapture, add to the moment by faking him out: Lean toward one nipple, lick it lightly, then surprise him by attacking the other one. Try variations on this theme, always keeping your man on edge. When it's finally time to move on, remember to say these two very important words: 'Your turn.' **"**

Turn Around

This section is a touchy one or one that many women don't want to touch. Anal stimulation can open both of you to another level of intense sexual sensations. Curt explains:

66 I think most straight men are curious about anal stimulation. They ask 'What does it feel like?' and 'Why do you like that?' Men are very curious about what it feels like, but they think if they desire it, that it means they're gay. 99

NOT! We often think of it as a gay thing, but my guys assure me that gay and straight butts are made the same. But anal sex is associated with gay men, and so some straight men feel funny trying it. Yet most straight men I interviewed expressed a desire for it and complain that women have an aversion to trying anal sex. There's tons of pleasure to be had from rear activities if both partners get over any hang-ups, which can be tough. Alex spells it out:

66 The biggest obstacle coming between men and pleasure is inhibition. Some men will not experiment sexually for the life of them. For example, the prostate gland in men is the seat of sexual pleasure. By stimulating this gland, sexual pleasure is increased greatly. Many men will not allow women to penetrate them because they think this will make them gay. It goes without saying that this is nonsense and that they're missing out on a great deal of pleasure. 99

"Most straight guys will say they're not into ass play, but we know the truth—pleasure is pleasure."   —Yiannis

The tush is a hotbed of nerves that can be stimulated in a variety of ways, for both sexes. You can lick or put lubrication on your finger and just rub it around the hole while giving a blowjob. Travis says anal stimulation during intercourse or oral sex can increase pleasure tenfold:

> I don't even know how to get a guy to go there, but play with his ass. Seriously. It's awesome, and if a guy can get over that whole finger-up-the-butt thing, he will be happy he did. Just make sure he is clean.

Orgasms that are enhanced by anal stimulation are way more intense, for both sexes. Yes, women enjoy anal stimulation too! A finger in the tush (he doesn't have to go up far) can stimulate the G-spot from the inside. Anal sex can be pleasurable too. Men like it because it's tighter than a vagina, so there's more stimulation. It has nothing to do with his sexuality. Women who try it often like it, if it doesn't hurt too much.

WARNING: Thoroughly clean ANYTHING that's been in the rectum before putting it anywhere else. Yiannis recommends:

> Get your man involved in a little ass play. Start off slowly, gradually inching your hands closer and closer to his opening during each sexual encounter. To create a positive association from

the start, the first time you actually touch it should be at a time when he is experiencing extreme pleasure. From there, let nature take its course. And, ladies, don't forget: In ballroom dance they say 'The best leader is a follower,' and never has that rule applied more than during anal sex. I wouldn't let a man inside of me who hadn't experienced it himself. 🙶

Anal muscles should be slowly stretched. If you try anal intercourse, always use a condom and LOTS of lubrication. Start SLOW. Try a finger, or several, first. If you're scared, make it clear that you're in charge. Back into him instead of him trying to thrust into you. Then you control the pace so your muscles relax more. You know you can stop if it hurts too much. It might take several tries to get used to it. Alex explains:

🙶 For women, I believe it only hurts the first couple of times unless the guy's really big. It's pleasurable because of the area that he's penetrating. Many men are afraid that something's going to come out. When you're in the vagina, it's not the case—you know nothing's gonna come out. So there are many psychological reservations that prohibit many men from actually experiencing it. It's definitely something to get beyond. 🙶

"Straight men need to get over it. Every straight guy I know who has actually let someone touch his prostate has bemoaned the fact that he waited so long."   — Michael T.F.

THE PROSTATE: The guys asked me to emphasize this—a lot. When it comes to anal stimulation, the prostate is the portal. Do you want to drive him crazy in bed? Get over squeamishness about stimulating the prostate, which can only be done through his butt. Help him get over his doubts and relax about it. Alex says it's not hard to find and stimulate the prostate, and the discomfort he may feel at first will leave as the pleasure takes over:

> 66 It's gonna be in one set place—not different from one man to the next, maybe slightly, but it's generally in the same area. Just go in there, and when he starts moaning and it feels good for him, you'll know. It's not necessarily the most comfortable thing for men. In some cases, he has to get beyond a certain bit of pain before he's able to enjoy it. 99

The prostate is the equivalent of our G-spot. Massaging it magnifies the other sensations he's experiencing. If you're giving him oral sex and use your finger too, it can greatly intensify his pleasure. If cleanliness is a concern for you, sex shops sell little rubbers that can cover a finger and protect it from any souvenirs. So how do you find the prostate? Michael T.F. says it's incredibly easy to find:

> 66 All you have to do is slip a well-lubricated finger into the rectum. The prostate is a walnut-size gland at the base of the penis. If you press the finger up (as in toward the stomach and not toward the back) you can't help but feel it. Rubbing the prostate, either alone or in combination with oral or manual sex, will make most men babble and promise you anything you want. 99

And if you still need a clearer picture, Curt adds:

66 Start between the balls and the butt hole, at the taint. If you start gently massaging that area, you may be amazed with where you'll go after. The prostate is underneath the taint. Pull a U-turn with your finger when you enter his butt. Pose your finger like you're holding a bowling ball. 99

"Lubrication is important. You may feel a power rush within yourself for doing it. You're penetrating a very sacred area." —Curt

Next time you go bowling, pay attention to how you hold the ball. It's a similar position for reaching his prostate. It's not hard to figure out. Sound any better? It really is worth a try!

Be His Fantasy

Most of us fantasize. Fantasies range from just envisioning yourself making love to your partner to wild scenarios that you probably want to leave in your mind. Couples handle fantasies in many ways. Too many don't acknowledge them to each other. Those who do say that it can enhance sex. Very often men fantasize about being with a woman who is assertive.

When you make unexpected moves on him, especially in a sexy outfit, you'll be his fantasy woman. A garter belt and stockings usually get extra points. And high heels. Leave the outfit on during sex for a while. It can make you feel sexier and in control. Hedda's point of view:

    " Nowadays, with porn and the sexual content on the Internet being so accessible, rules about sex have changed. It is partly true that to keep your man you have to act like a porn star to please him. Actually, a women needs to act like an aggressive gay man in bed. No inhibitions! Experimentation is a plus, and sex toys are a necessity to keep your visually overstimulated man pleased and your sex life on track. "

> "Be the one to initiate sex too."   —David

Most men love a whore in bed. He loves you—his sweetheart out of bed—being his whore in the sack. There's nothing like someone who is very ladylike in public becoming wild and uninhibited in bed. Nothing! So once you feel comfortable with him and trust him not to judge you, nurture your inner whore and be his fantasy. It will get you much more in the mood for sex too. It's best with someone you've been with for a while.

Bring out your inner whore by being open-minded. Ask what he'd like you to wear, and accommodate him with what you feel comfortable doing. There's a world of options once you let go of generic beliefs. Being a whore can be fun! According to Patrick:

    " Men are visually stimulated and crave variety. Try to find out what his fantasy is, and bring it to life for him—within reason.

Keep the visual appeal there from time to time with the use of lingerie, sex toys, corsets, wigs, bold makeup, crotchless leather
panties, Catholic schoolgirl skirts, whatever. It may take a while to
find out what your man's triggers are—and just how far he'll be
willing to go to indulge his and your fantasies—but the idea is to
keep the excitement there by trying new things. 🙶

"Free your mind and his crotch will follow."   —Michael A.

If he shares a fantasy that you could easily play out with him,
consider doing it. Sometimes a woman may go to a bar and let her
guy make believe he's picking her up. Harmless ones like that may
bring sexy nights! But, as David warns, there should be balance, as
with everything else in relationships:

🙶 I don't think fantasies should be the basis of a sexual relationship, though. That should be the interaction and chemistry
between two people. It should not be based on working out fantasies. That's like a fire that's going to burn out. 🙶

Don't talk about your fantasies unless you feel very comfortable
with your guy. And don't ask him about his unless you can handle
what he says. If you expect him to say he fantasizes about making
love to you on a desert isle, you'll be very disappointed, and possibly disgusted, if he tells you he dreams of making love to five
women in public and you're not one of them. Vinnie admits:

> **66** I'd be very careful to advise a girl to ask a guy what his fantasies are unless she really wants to hear them. I guarantee it's not going to be running through the park or a vanilla bondage thing. It will be something dark. **99**

Fantasy isn't reality. Just because he thinks about something doesn't mean he really wants to do it. Often a fantasy is just for mind use—something to think about to get aroused. It can turn him on in thought. For example, if he fantasizes about an actress, he knows he will never meet her, but it still helps with arousal. And you might get unnecessarily jealous if he shares it, so it's just for his mind. Fantasies turn us on. You should have your own. Use fantasies to get into the mood. Create some together, and if you're both comfortable act some out. But the word to remember is BOTH. If you're doing it just to please him, DON'T! Just try to be open-minded to some new stuff that doesn't feel offensive to you. Michael A. recommends creating fantasies with him:

> **66** Share fantasy storytelling. First he says something; then you add something. For example, 'She walked into the room with a tennis dress and there's a line of sweat down his back.' He would write that down and hand it to you. You fill out the next step. 'She threw down her racket and unzipped her dress.' This way you create your own shared fantasy, and in a subtle way you can tell each other what turns you on. If something comes up that's uncomfortable, you can change it in what you write next. You can have some fun with fantasies but also set limits. **99**

"After you've been with someone for a while, you always should bring out toys."   —David

Try some toys if he's open to that. Vibrators aren't just for us. They stimulate guys too. Take turns using one all over each other's bodies. Go to a sex shop together and pick up stuff that looks like fun. Go slowly and keep "fun" as your operative word.

Toys may make him feel inadequate. "Why do you need a vibrator if you can have me?" Because it feels great. It's a different kind of stimulation. Don't use a regular vibrator in the back door or it can vibrate up and up and up. There are vibrators for anal stimulation with stoppers that prevent them from going in too far. You both can try one. Alex adds:

66 Toys can intimidate him. Many men, if not most straight men, have a thing in their heads that doesn't allow them to see themselves putting anything up their rectums. Some men just don't like that, period. Before the toys are brought into the bedroom, a man's mentality should be one of exploration. Men and women should be willing to explore together, both interested in trying new things. If they don't have that mentality, they can't do anything of that nature. So when that's established, bring the toys on and have a ball. 99

The same applies to porn. Sexy movies can turn you on if you stop worrying that your bod doesn't cut it next to the on-screen chick. Trust me, I've talked to enough men who are stymied about why we worry so much. He watches her for stimulation but wants to make love to YOU. He's not comparing you to the on-screen women. If you're very sensual in your touch and movements, that's what he'll eat up. So, relax and enjoy!

First-Aid Tips

- Bring your vibrator into bed with him.
- Find something to compliment about your guy in bed.
- Look in the mirror and say "Damn, I'm hot, and he's lucky to have me!"

Putting the "Self" Back in Self-Esteem

Tools for Becoming a Self-Empowered Woman

"I am amazed at how much I keep learning and trying to improve myself. That A+ is still a ways off."

—Mike

Do you want a partner who makes you happy on many levels? If you answered yes, please accept that the ONLY way to fix men, or anyone else, is to fix yourself. If a guy treats you in unacceptable ways, ignoring how it makes you feel leads only to pain. When you're healthy on the inside, it shows and helps weed damaged people out of your life. Those worth keeping will respond well to the "new you." Those who aren't good for you won't. Being completely satisfied with who you are or confident in yourself is easier said than done, says Vinnie, who also has struggled with this issue:

 My mother once told me 'Just be yourself.' That sounds so simple, but it's not. You can spend a lifetime trying to live in your own skin. But if you can do that, you'll be more attractive and won't have to worry about eliciting a response from someone. I was with a guy for a long time and spent a lot of time trying to figure out what he wanted me to be like. I should have spent that time working on me. If we're smart, we end up doing that. **"**

"It's a whole lot easier to fix yourself instead of him, and the change will be permanent and genuine."   **—Michael A.**

We've discussed the importance of accepting men as they are and operating from that acceptance. Now we hope to convince you to accept yourself. Until you do, prepare to settle for bits of happiness instead of the whole enchilada. I encourage you to get into oink mode and go after all of the happiness you deserve. When you change your ways and take care of yourself first, you face men from a point of power. But, as Michael M. points out, this takes time and work on your part:

" You can't just go out and get self-esteem. They don't sell it at Kmart. You have to find it inside of you and develop it. I'm sure deep down even the biggest stars in the world don't feel like they're worth it on some level. **"**

"Realize that you are the superior sex."   **—Randall**

Feeling Whole Without a Man

If your self-esteem comes from a man, you're nothing without one. If you no longer need one to feel whole, you'll be more comfortable waiting to meet someone who's worthy of you. Good self-esteem is a power tool like no other. Having it allows you to truly control your own power. It begins with giving yourself REAL love, not just love lip service. Alex explains:

“ As often as we hear about the importance of loving yourself, it does not filter through to some women. It is so difficult to do. Many women shrug it off and say 'Yes, I love myself,' but it's the same women who are beating themselves up for not having their hair right or for a feature they don't like. These insecurities weigh them down. Then they just casually shrug it off and say "I love myself," but they don't! You need to really evaluate whether you're living up to that. Until you can truly look at yourself in the mirror and say 'I love myself,' you shouldn't be in a relationship. As long as you continue to keep a focus on that when in a relationship, you're fine. ”

> "You can't make men your priority. It's not always bad to be a little selfish!"
> —Kyle

While you don't have to avoid relationships until you're perfect, you should get a head start before your next guy. Look in the mirror often and say "I love you." It can be hard, but if you persist it gets easier, and eventually it sinks in. You've heard it often, but it's so true—you can't get good loving from someone if you don't give it to yourself. How can you show yourself love?

Learning to Love Yourself

Treating yourself more lovingly focuses on YOU. Each loving action is a reminder that you deserve to be happy and pampered. As you act a bit more self-loving, self-appreciation increases as you enjoy the goodies you allow for you. Become conscious of how you can be good to yourself. It sets a tone for others too. Accept that, as a unique human being, you matter! Fritz emphasizes:

> 66 You need to like yourself more. Stop listening to a little voice in your head that says you're not good enough, and start listening to the even littler one that says that you matter. Make sure to look your absolute best. Do the most with what you've been given in life, but don't obsess on it. There are so many other things about a person that make them special that make them matter. 99

David suggests making the time to pamper yourself:

> 66 A lot of women can't afford to go to a day spa, but you can get a manicure and pedicure almost anywhere for a good price. Get your hair done on a regular basis. Get a scrub and a mask at a drugstore. Deep condition your hair. Spend a night just taking care of you. Make yourself look and feel beautiful. If you

do things like this to pamper yourself, you'll feel better about you. **99**

Develop more appreciation for your inner attributes. It's a happy process that should never end. Become conscious of your details. Often you're the only one who notices your faults. Cellulite can cloud vision. It's hard to see what you can appreciate if you dwell on what you don't like. Get others to point out your good details. They're more important than perceived flaws. Rick says:

66 Real self-reflection is one of the best ways to develop self-esteem. Write a list of your attributes that make you as valuable as you are. Look at that list every day and add to that list every day. The more you check in with that list, the better you'll feel about yourself. **99**

"It sounds corny, but God made us perfect as we are. I really believe that. It's a fantasy to think that someone can complete you. We are all complete."   —Vinnie

Keep adding to your list. It just takes time to accept it. Pay attention to your good qualities and read the list often. Self-esteem begins with saying "I accept myself as I am." If you keep saying it, eventually it sinks in. As you get to know you, work on making the most of what you have. Glenn highly recommends:

“ Stop looking at magazines and comparing the models to you! The other day some drop-dead gorgeous girl came in. She showed me a picture of Britney Spears while telling me how she wanted her hair but was pointing at Britney's face. That's not realistic. Find your best attributes and work with them. Don't listen to what everyone else says. ”

If you feel the need to self-criticize, Michele suggests you look at yourself—at what works and what doesn't.

“ Think positive. Invest more in developing what works so you can get the most power out of it. Eventually you will have the strength to improve the part of yourself you don't like. ”

It may sound crazy, but you control how people see you, at least to a degree. Attitude rules, and you can develop a positive, confident one. Changing your self-perception can make you come across as more attractive. It's YOUR choice to let things that you don't like rule how you see yourself. You can build your confidence by working with what you have. Kevin A. advises:

“ Work out, go to the gym, go to the salon, buy a dress, and watch Oprah. I know women who are overweight but are comfortable with who they are, so men call them all the time. ”

You can control the perception of who you are. When you're deliciously curvaceous instead of fat, men appreciate your body a lot more. Let a confident attitude define you. Be kinder to yourself. Don't look for what you can criticize. Pay more attention to your wonderful qualities. I asked the guys to share any specific things a woman can do to improve her self-esteem. Carl suggests:

> 66 Yoga, meditation, therapy, exercise, art class, shopping, whatever it takes! Many people, both men and women, battle with low self-esteem. Realize that you're not alone, and find out what activities make you a more confident individual. 99

In addition, when you experience the joy of making someone's life better—not the guy who takes you for granted but someone who truly benefits from what you give and shows appreciation—you feel better about yourself too. Rick adds:

> 66 Nothing makes anybody feel more beautiful or better about themselves than stepping outside of themselves and helping others. There is nothing like a good dose of looking around and seeing people who are less fortunate or need your help. When you feel you really have something to give, you can't help but feel more beautiful. So get outside of yourself, step away from the mirror, take a look around, and see what needs doing. That boosts confidence, takes you outside of yourself, and makes you feel that you're doing something worthwhile. You become more beautiful inside, and that keeps blossoming. 99

"Do something for someone else. Help a charity. That's a great way to boost your self-esteem because you're needed by other people."   —Fritz

Make Yourself Feel Beautiful

Can you see your own beauty, or do you need it pointed out? Self-appreciation, especially about your appearance, is a tough commodity to have these days. We gush about men who make us feel beautiful. Often all that matters is what HE thinks. You can look in the mirror and think you look good. But if he doesn't compliment your appearance, your self-image can sink fast. Ed advises:

66 Learn to be comfortable with yourself and not need reinforcement from someone else. Learn to love what God gave you. And then learn to WORK IT! And if you REALLY want to know the TRUTH, which you usually don't when asking questions about how you look or how good you are, ask your girlfriends, and by that I would include gay men. But you REALLY better be ready for the TRUTH at that point! **99**

"My shrink used to say if finding a man is a lucky thing, then luck is the residual of careful planning, and that planning should be about making yourself the best."   —Vinnie

We often can't handle the truth, be it good or bad. If he says something nice, you think he's just saying it to please you. If he gives a negative answer, you feel worse. We often ask those dumb questions like "Do I look fat?" because we're so insecure that we need him to tell us we're wonderful. But if you don't feel good about yourself, there's little he can say that will make a difference past the first minutes after he says something nice. Michael A. warns:

> **"** It's a subtle way of manipulating him into giving the right answer. You're forcing him to lie and reinforcing the idea that there's something wrong with your body. There isn't! **"**

Catch yourself before you ask a question to get reinforcement for your appearance. The response probably won't bring the results you want. Vinnie warns:

> **"** Don't ask a question if you don't want to hear the answer—either answer. That golden rule applied when my mother asked me if I am gay, and it applies here. Being truthful with somebody is a sign of respect, in my book, so don't take it out on your boyfriend—or anybody—if he doesn't give you the answer you want. What you should be doing is going around saying 'Tell me I don't look fat,' if that's what you want to hear. **"**

Those questions are often lose/lose situations. And men HATE them! They know there are no good answers. It's time to stop looking to others to confirm that you're beautiful. Take control of your perception. Beauty is in the eye of the beholder!—even if the beholder is yourself. If you feel beautiful on your own, HE can't take it away. That's hard. It takes time and a conscious desire—and self-acceptance, which can blossom into a radiant confidence that makes you more attractive. Kevin S. says:

> 66 It all comes from within—from being happy by yourself. You have to do that yourself. Stop trying to be somebody you're not. Realize what you are and what your positive qualities are. You cannot invent someone else for you. You have to attract people and be attractive, and I don't mean just in a physical way. I think there are people who are sure of themselves and could get up in the morning and not need all this intricate care. They have a simple approach to life and love daily life. These are the people that people are attracted to. 99

> "Women overanalyze! They often examine their own looks, tastes, needs, attitudes, habits, and material possessions to make sure they measure up to the idealized woman they think they ought to be. Instead of being self-confident, they magnify their own flaws."   —Bob

Your attitude sets a tone for how beautiful you feel. Confidence is THE most attractive quality to nurture in you. Women who constantly need reinforcement turn guys off. It's a burden that frustrates them about what to say. A confident woman comes across as much more attractive. Taking care of your needs will help you relax about men, and that translates into being more appealing to them, says Vinnie:

" Being secure in the fact that you are complete just as you are is so attractive and sexy. You won't have to go on a manhunt. Men will be knocking down the door. There's nothing sexier than a person who is comfortable in his or her own skin. "

I am by no means thin or young, but I feel youthful, hot, and sexy, and it radiates from me. Develop your own glow by working from within. Fake it until it's real. Eventually you may not notice when you go from acting confident to owning it. Practice makes it real! Kyle couldn't agree more:

" A woman's power lies in her self-confidence and faith in herself. If you truly believe that you can do anything, you can. This confidence allows you to do whatever you want. If you believe in yourself, anything is possible. "

"I think attraction is in how sensual you feel, which is inside, not outside. It's not youth or makeup; it's feeling good inside and conveying that."   —Mike

Compliments are like Band-Aids. You elicit some kind words out of HIM, and for the moment you're assuaged. But the glow rarely lasts long. Forcing him to answer uncomfortable questions doesn't do it either. The only way to feel consistently lovely is to accept all the beauty that is you, without diminishing it with what you feel you "should" be. Travis urges:

❝ Stop comparing yourself. I know I am never going to look like Paul Walker—but God bless him, because he is hot!—so why try to change myself to look like him, or the guy on the box of Calvin Klein underwear? Don't change to try to fit some society-determined fad. Change to be the person you want to be. I play softball every week, but am not the best batter in the world—far from it, to tell the truth. I work out to get stronger so I can hit the ball farther. The benefit is I end up with a nice chest, shoulders, and arms. So change because you want to change, not because you think it's what everyone else wants. ❞

Comparisons are useless! We're all individuals. Someone will always have qualities that you don't. Why feel bad? What they have or look like or do well at takes nothing away from you, unless YOU allow it to. Often the media creates the standard. Few can achieve that. Plus, most people you see in the media don't look nearly as good in real life! You can only work with what you have on a realistic level.

"We all need to work on ourselves—for ourselves. Improving yourself in a healthy, constructive manner enhances your life and outlook. And in the end, though you did it for yourself, you end up being more attractive to just about everyone because of it."   **—Andy**

Tips for Feeling Beautiful

Beauty begins with your perception of how you look. If what you don't like is most important, you'll never feel beautiful. If you make the most of your assets and nurture yourself, your inner beauty shines through and makes the outside bloom. According to Kyle, find at least one thing about you that you feel is sexy:

   ❝ There is nothing that gives more self-confidence than being able to realize that you are sexy and have something about you that others desire. You don't necessarily need to use it all the time, but it's important that you know you have it. **❞**

We all have sexy qualities, if we open our eyes to them. Making your nice qualities more important than flaws helps you say "I love you!" in the mirror with conviction. Do it no matter how you feel. The more you say it, the faster it will sink in! Giving yourself love, taking excellent care of your health, and consciously appreciating your good attributes lead to stronger self-appreciation. Jason explains:

   ❝ It's in the way you carry yourself: exercise, eat right, take care of your skin and your hair, and choose your clothes. After a while people give up if they haven't found the right guy. I don't go out to the supermarket if it's not the right outfit. The right guy might be there. **❞**

The more well groomed you are, the better you feel. You can also change your self-perception by using kinder words toward yourself. Referring to yourself as "fat" is out! If you gain a little weight, you're rounder, not disgustingly fatter. Let your inner glow temper imperfections. We're always much tougher on ourselves than we are on others. Pay more attention to good qualities, and keep it real. Yiannis suggests:

> ❝ You should definitely make an effort to highlight the things that make you beautiful, but don't make yourself into something you're not. If you normally wear sneakers, leave the six-inch stilettos in the closet. Usually go fragrance free? Now is not the time to try out J-Lo's latest perfume. You're going to be judged against the impression you make during those first few months of the relationship, so make sure you're being yourself. ❞

> "Too much fingernails and pasting on the fake stuff don't attract men or attract the wrong men. Men are looking for a woman to be a real person, not this wrapped-up thing."   **—Kevin S.**

The consensus among the guys is that you can make yourself beautiful in many ways by using tools that are available. Many of the guys said that seeing a woman who's sloppily dressed, looking like she's done nothing to look nice, makes you look like you don't care about yourself and probably have low self-esteem. Attention to your appearance increases confidence. Take care of your hair. A good cut can enhance your appearance. And as you get older, you may want to think about taking advantage of innovations in hair color. Kevin S.'s professional opinion:

> **"** I think gray hair on a lot of people is not attractive. Ask yourself 'Do I have the type of hair that looks good gray?' Normally, wiry and curly hair does not look good gray. Gray does not look so bad on people with straighter hair. Fuzzy gray hair does not help anyone. Tint or color your hair. There is a world of nonperoxide colors over the counter. In beauty salons you have to ask if they use them. You can match them to your natural color. That helps you look more youthful, which has to make you feel better about yourself. And highlights are fabulous. They perk everybody up, if they're done right. **"**

> "Stop looking in the mirror so much in the middle of the day when no one is around. You have to work on that in a mental way."
>
> —Kevin S.

A little makeup can go a long way to improve how you feel about you. You may feel perkier if you dress for an event and use makeup to enhance your appearance. Make sure your clothes fit properly and flatter you. When you dress like a bum to run errands, you don't want to bump into anyone. Why feel like that? Try to make yourself look reasonably nice every day, even if you're not going anywhere special. What if you bump into an ex-boyfriend? It's blissful to be wearing clothes that work when you see someone you know. You'll enjoy the extra confidence that helps you look him in the eye and smile, instead of ducking into an alley so he doesn't see you in your unflattering duds. Flattering clothes do wonders. Kevin K. says many things can help you feel more beautiful:

> ❝ Some fabrics, such as silk, are made for feeling beautiful. Also, experiment with fragrance and color. I think a person feels not beautiful mostly because of self-neglect. We are often socialized into such self-neglect by messages from advertisers and others who would have us feel insufficient or second-class. Creating beautiful, romantic settings helps since we tend to take on the mood of our surroundings. ❞

> "My number-one rule is to make sure that your shoes are up to date. Have the high heels and swingbacks and everything. You must have shoes, shoes, shoes, shoes, shoes!"   —**Kevin A.**

You have to be careful about what you wear as you get older, adds Kevin S.:

> ❝ You cannot pile layers and layers of clothing all over your body, or you become this walking monolith. You're bigger than life, like a bigger billboard, and it intimidates men. A simpler approach to your clothing as you get older is so smart. Puh-leez, be more classic as you get older. ❞

Improving Body Image

The biggest self-esteem buster for women is body image. Many of us can never be thin enough. There's always something wrong—that pound you think you must lose to be perfect; cellulite that only you see; a wee bit too large to fit into size four. What an injustice to your body! Curves are lovely. So are natural breasts, large or small. The worst is a perception that you should be thinner than most of us are meant to be. That creates poor eating habits and/or self-hatred or at least insecurity. If you don't feel good about your body, it inhibits confidence about your ability to attract a special guy. I implore you to reconsider how thin and perfect your body should be. Travis understands our plight because it's common not just in women:

> 66 I just wrote a column all about gay men and their body image issues, so I have some strong feelings on this. Ladies, if you think guys are judging you, you should try living in the gay world, filled with gym queens who spend hours a day at the gym to have the perfect body so they can go out and dance with their shirts off. Better yet, go into a gay store and look at everything from the underwear that is for sale to greeting cards. EVERYTHING has a shirtless guy on it, and if that's not enough to put your self-image in doubt, I don't know what is. Even in the gay newspaper that I write for, I saw ads for lawyers with their shirts off because apparently if a guy is willing to work hard to have a six-pack, he is going to work just as hard to represent me in court or whatever! 99

> "The reality is that most guys like curves. Few want to actually screw a starving runway model."   —Andy

There's a lot of pressure to reach a certain body standard. The media shows airbrushed women who we're supposed to look like. Please learn to live with what you've got. Celebrities pay thousands, and hundreds of thousands, to create their "perfect" looks. Striving for that isn't fair to you. Do what you can to improve without letting it affect your confidence. Patrick says:

    " We're just as bad, if not worse, than straight women in this regard. If you're good at conditioning yourself, just relax and remind yourself that you will lose those pounds eventually. Reward yourself with a non-food item when you do. **"**

Take control of your body—not for HIM but for you. Experience the pleasure of being able to control your eating instead of getting the instant gratification of something fattening that ends with the last bite. Pay attention to how you eat, and why. Then see what you can do to improve yourself. David suggests:

    " If food is an issue, look at your diet. If you don't feel good about yourself, you have to figure out what makes you feel that way. It's different for everybody. Make sure that you're doing what you can to make yourself look better. **"**

"Do you think HE is stressing out over a few pounds? Then why should you?"   —Michael T.F.

It's also very important to feel like you're taking control by getting exercise. Going on a power walk can make you feel on top of the world. Exercise is powerful. It reduces stress and actually gives you more energy. Burning calories is a lovely extra. If you're allergic to exercise, find a hypoallergenic way to get your butt moving. Exercise is critical to your well-being, not just to lose weight, and there are plenty of ways to get it—so there's NO excuse not to.

"Exercise makes your body better, ups your endorphins, makes your skin better, and gives you less time to worry about what's not happening in your life."   —Kevin A.

When you feel needy for a man, walk or run. Raise your endorphins. Unless you have a physical ailment that prevents it, exercise is something you CAN control. Actually doing it can up your self-esteem dramatically. Take a walk. Go up and down stairs at home or work often. Jump rope. Do jumping jacks. The benefits of exercise far surpass just losing weight. Focus on doing it for the health benefits—a healthier heart, stronger bones, lower stress, stronger body, and so on. And last but not least, Randy advises:

   ❝ Hang around with gay men who treat you with the respect and admiration you deserve. Even at their well-meaning best, straight men forget to compliment a woman on her hair, her clothes, her new purse or fabulous dress. Flattery just isn't part of their genetic makeup, which means you must look for validation elsewhere. Remember: Gay men don't want to get in your pants. They only want to tell you how great you look in them. **"**

First-Aid Tips

- Buy yourself roses and accentuate your environment with pretty scents, mood music, and good lighting.
- List everything that you can control in your life if you choose to, including allowing yourself to splurge on the best cheesecake in your hometown.
- Work on developing the qualities in yourself first that you want in a man.

A FEW FINAL WORDS

*"We are meant to be loved and loving, vulnerable
and warm, dependent and independent."*
—*Vinnie*

I hope that the guys and I made you think about what you truly
want from a relationship and convinced you that learning to control
your need for a romantic partner will make your life much richer.
Having gay friends will also enrich your life! Getting to know these
guys was a delight for me! They're sweet and accommodating and
were willing to help me in ways I rarely encounter with straight
women and men. Michael A. says:

❝ Gay men represent a different version of the owner's
manual for straight women. They have the same equipment and
mentality but no agenda. That's what makes us so good as a
sounding board for straight women. ❞

Gay friends will give you straight advice in ways that your girlfriends probably can't—in a direct and practical way. But they do it with your best interest in mind, not to be catty or to take out their rage against men on your guy. The characters on *Will & Grace* illustrated the benefits of having gay friends and how they can add a lovely dimension to your life. And having them will probably get you more compliments, encouragement, and love than you get now. Michael T.F. says he has always been exposed to the needs of women:

> 66 I was raised by women and have always surrounded myself with female friends, so I've seen firsthand all the unfortunate things they do when men enter the picture. I think if every girl were told she's the most important thing in the world when she's growing up and every boy were made to realize he isn't, things would be better for everyone. 99

We want you to be happy and hope that you'll do whatever you can to appreciate who you are. It's the greatest gift you can give to YOU. Gay friends can help you feel special by pointing out why you are. Most understand that it's nice to help friends feel good about themselves. Of course you should be a good friend back! While they're good at giving advice, the guys assured me they experience the same problems that women do and make many of the same mistakes. Patrick adds:

> 66 As a general caveat, remember: Though your gay male friends may dish out the relationship advice with aplomb, straight

women and gay men are not merely simpatico in sexual preference. They are subject to making the same stupid mistakes. Heed
their advice with a grain of salt and your own intuition, making
sure to give it back when you see them falling headfirst into the
arms of some queer cretin. **"**

We hope that you take away from this book the fact that only you
can make your life better. Only you can change how a guy treats
you. Only you can control your need for a man. And only you can
make yourself receptive to a healthy relationship. You have the
power to control YOU, which in turn elicits more satisfying
responses from others. If you give up everything for a man, you'll
stick with him for better or worse, and it will probably be worse.
When you develop a life that's not dependent on anyone, it gets better and better. There's less stress since you can stay with him if it's
good or return to enjoying your life without him if he makes you
complain more than you smile.

"Be yourself and never let him take over. Never lose sight of your
goals. I know so many women who give up their creative side
when they fall in love. Don't!"   —Mike

Don't put your life into a guy's hands. Maintain it always, even
if you're married! It's good to have your own friends and interests.
I used to revolve around every man I was involved with and settled
for bits of joy amid the drama I complained about, until my gay
hairdresser got through to me.

Having been on both sides, I can attest that being happy on my own attracts healthier guys, allows me to enjoy doing things solo, and helps me pass on men who aren't worth giving up other things for. And I now accept that men have a right to be who they are and appreciate it. Men do appreciate our differences when they're not being inundated with nagging and demands! Matthew explains:

> 66 Men have many strengths. But they also have many weaknesses. This is talking in broad terms, but men don't understand their own feelings and other things that women really do. Men and women need each other—they balance and complement each other. Your attributes and strengths are just as valuable as men's are. 99

I wake up smiling every day because I know I'm happy with or without a romantic partner. It's fun to share experiences with a special guy. It's also fun to plan time around what suits you best. When I'm solo, I enjoy doing what I want, when I want, how I want. But it's fun to get all dolled up for a date with him. It's also fun not to care about appearance for a day and laze around in bed watching old movies wearing granny underwear and no makeup. It's fun to make love to him. It's also fun to make love to yourself. Kyle advises:

> 66 Just enjoy your life no matter what guy you're with or not with. If you can have fun with your guy—great. If you have fun solo or with friends—great. No one brings happiness into your life if you're not happy on your own. Once you are, everything can be fun if you allow it to be! Learn to see the benefits of all situations. 99

Seek relationships that are two-way streets instead of you doing all the giving. While you shouldn't settle for a man, get realistic in your expectations of what you need from a romantic partner. Nobody is perfect. People in great relationships fight but work out problems because they love each other. They don't become shrews or bail at the first sign of a flaw. Decide what's most important in a guy. Does he treat you with respect, show you love, act supportively, and try in a reasonable way to make you happy? That's crucial to have! But many things we want aren't. Michael A. lovingly implores:

> **❝** Stop trying to change men. We are fundamentally different, and it's actually that difference that makes it so adventurous and fun. I've always thought of women as airplanes. An airplane needs a long tarmac to get airborne. A man is more like a rocket. He goes straight up. They both reach the same heights but in completely different ways. When an airplane tries to make a rocket into an airplane, it's not possible mentally, emotionally, or physically. So just wave from 30,000 feet. And when you land, you can have fun. But in the meantime, don't try to put airplane parts into the rocket because it ain't going to work! **❞**

Accept that men won't be everything you expect, and that's okay. Distinguish between annoying and bad behavior. Is he not the best dresser? Does he prefer playing video games over going to the theater? Is he slower than you at chores? Does he not read your mind in bed? Not deal breakers!

Stop waiting for a prince to sweep you off your feet! Good reasons to leave are he's overly critical, expects you to do everything for him, doesn't keep his word, lies, abuses you mentally or physically, and/ or cheats. Create your own concept of a healthy relationship that includes his foibles and annoying ways. I'm sure you have some too!

"Every day doesn't have to be glorious. A relationship is not like a movie where every minute is like light and champagne in front of the Eiffel Tower. There are bad days like anything else. As long as overall it's an overwhelming thumbs-up, it's a good situation."

—Michael M.

Once you develop a life, the rest falls into place easier. I'm finishing this book on the deck at the Denali Wilderness Lodge in Alaska, looking at the mountain I hiked up yesterday. This is the most remote lodge in the United States—thirty-five miles from the nearest road. I flew in a bush plane to get here, which I'd never done, and saw views from that great experience that I couldn't even imagine. Alaska has always been my dream, so I decided to have a Solo Chick Alaska Adventure (for details, my blog is www. solochickalaska.blogspot.com). No worries about men or getting permission. As I traveled through Alaska solo I went kayaking, canoeing, on a speedboat safari, and hiking a lot—when it suited ME. It was a perfect trip for a single chick who loves the outdoors.

Years ago I could never have done any of this, but now I've learned the joy of making dreams come true. This lodge is true Alaska with the comforts of home, and I got to be here because I CHOSE to pursue dreams instead of men (who I'll let find me!). It's inspiring to know that I'm deep in the heart of the Alaskan wilderness, surrounded by trees and mountains, yet in a comfy cabin—a spectacular place for me to write! On this trip I am so busy being happy that I never wonder where I can go to find men. I encourage you to find your own passions and go after them. Life is abundant with joy when you take charge of your life! Give yourself that blessing.

> "Get a life so you have a better sense of who you are. Do an overall maintenance. Work on looking and feeling as good as you can. It will make you feel more secure."   —Glenn

Sarah Bernhardt said, "Life begets life. Energy creates energy. It is by spending oneself that one becomes rich." Go out and spend yourself! Discover what things make you happy that don't involve a guy and pursue them with a vengeance. Find the kind of joy that I find in Alaska. Target your passion and spend time planning ways to own it. It doesn't have to be huge. You might want to catch up on books you haven't allowed time for or take a painting class. Allow yourself to dream and know that dreams can become real if you want them to. Use the energy for making YOU happy that you otherwise put into finding men and making them happy. Trust that when you're ready, a good man will find his way to you.

It's been our pleasure to help enlighten you about how to be happier, with or without a man. When you turn the suggestions into actions, I hope you discover why I wake up smiling every day. We wish you a happy and blessed journey toward discovering the joys of having a good life that revolves around YOU.

INDEX

proclaiming, in spite of men's actions, 79–82

Luongo, Mike, 9–10
   on avoiding abusive behavior, 55–56
   on expecting to be treated well, 153
   on expressing yourself in bed, 245–46
   on living for the moment, 150
   on men's desire to please women sexually, 252
   on men's expressiveness, 109
   on mystery in a relationship, 164
   on needing a life outside of love, 41
   on not losing sight of your goals, 311
   on oral sex, 274
   on self-confidence, 299
   on self-improvement, 289
   on teaching men about romance, 134
   on touching, 270
   on watching for contradictions in behavior, 58

lying, 86–89

M

Make Money, Not Excuses: Wake Up, Take Charge, and Overcome Your Financial Fears Forever (Chatsky), 199–200

male behavior, accepting, 172–74

male cave, 99

male conflict, on type of woman desired, 228–30

manhunts, 14–16, 28–29

manipulation, 58, 74, 119–24

mantraps, designing apartments as, 12

marriage
   obsession with, 215–18
   putting into perspective, 209–26

masturbation, 253–56

Matthews, Dan, 8
   on being alone, 203
   on camaraderie between straight women and gay men, 3
   on desperation, 20
   on the excitement of attraction, 162–63
   on jealousy, 171
   on remaining open minded about men, 24
   on role-playing in bad relationships, 59–60
   on traits of happy women, 46
   on trying to change men, 94

McDerman, Michael, 9
   on accepting people, 97
   on accepting sex as natural, 244
   on advice from girlfriends, 104–5
   on attitude toward sexuality, 252
   on avoiding parent/child-type communication, 112
   on being a single mom, 221
   on being yourself, 240
   on commitment issues, 225
   on communicating about sex, 246
   on communication and boundaries, 176
   on complimenting a man for his appearance, 185
   on differences between men's and women's communication, 108–9
   on dressing for the first date, 167
   on emotionally available men, 170
   on finding balanced independence, 45
   on game playing, 142
   on getting what you want from a man, 183
   on keeping relationships at a slower pace, 84
   on living for the moment, 151
   on looking for money in a relationship, 213
   on men not completing women, 34

solitude, benefits of, 194

space
  creating for others, 181
  valuing one's own, 143–44

spirituality, 205–7

Stuart, Jason, 8
  on beginning a relationship, 162, 165
  on calling men, 149
  on communicating about sex, 249
  on deciding to have sex, 233
  on forgetting past lessons, 195
  on getting to know somebody, 155
  on hiring people to help, 199
  on how women are raised, 138
  on men's two-facedness, 126
  on presenting yourself, 301
  on recognizing responsibility, 64
  on relaxing during sex, 257
  on role playing during sex, 267
  on sexual insecurity, 237
  on the voices in your head, 258
  on women's sexual assertiveness, 239

Sullivan, Carl, 8
  on accepting late invites, 145
  on compromise, 179–80
  on condoms, 128
  on dressing for the first date, 166
  on financial independence, 200
  on getting help around the house, 184
  on improving self-esteem, 295
  on keeping desire for marriage in
    perspective, 215
  on Mr. Right, a realist take, 19
  on not being completed by
    someone else, 38
  on pressure to have children, 219–20
  on Prince Charming, 73
  on seeking balance, 27
  on the thrill of the chase, 82–83
  on trying to change men, 94

T

taking your time, at the beginning of a
  relationship, 159–63

tenderness, 124–27

testosterone imperative, 117, 121

time, sense of, different between men
  and women, 173

touching, 269–70

Trabucco, Rick, 10
  on autonomy, 42, 44
  on avoiding extreme reactions at the
    beginning of a relationship, 84–85
  on being alone, 204
  on being nice and naughty, 242
  on cat-and-mouse relationship, 146
  on commitment phobia, 226
  on defining love, 80
  on devaluing one's worth, 32
  on differences between men and
    women, 105
  on the effects of spirituality, 206
  on faking orgasms, 251
  on friendship as basis for healthy
    relationship, 157
  on friendships, importance of, 202
  on getting outside yourself, 295
  on good friends, 158
  on having a healthy relationship
    with yourself, 192
  on jealousy, 172
  on looking at yourself as the
    prize, 140
  on making excuses for men's
    bad behavior, 77
  on manhunts, 15
  on masturbation, 256
  on men learning romance, 132
  on men saying what women want
    to hear, 78

ABOUT THE AUTHOR

Daylle Deanna Schwartz is a personal growth counselor, speaker, and author of many books, including the bestselling *All Men Are Jerks Until Proven Otherwise* and *How to Please a Woman In & Out of Bed*. She also publishes a free e-newsletter, *Self-Empowerment Quarterly*. Daylle is regularly quoted in national consumer magazines, including the *New York Times, Cosmopolitan,* and *Marie Claire*. She also appears as an expert on television and radio shows, including *Oprah, Good Morning America, Inside Edition, Howard Stern,* and *Montel Williams*. She resides in New York City. Visit her at www.daylle.com.

Take off your blinders!

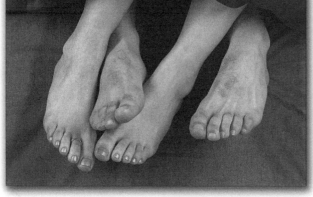